ARGUMENTATION
— AND —
DEBATE
A STRATEGIC PERSPECTIVE

KENNETH E. TROYER
GARY G. HARMON
DR. DAVID C. BAILEY

Argumentation & Debate
—A Strategic Perspective

Copyright © 2016 Kenneth E. Troyer, Gary G. Harmon, and Dr. David C. Bailey

Published by BookRipple
www.BookRipple.com

All rights reserved. No part of this book may be reproduced or transmitted in any form or by any means, electronic or mechanical, including photocopying and recording, or by an information storage and retrieval system, without permission in writing from the authors.

ISBN: 978-1-943157-31-0
Printed in the United States of America

Contents

CHAPTER ONE:
  Introduction to Argumentation   5

CHAPTER TWO:
  Basic Argument Theory   14

CHAPTER THREE:
  Fact Debate   56

CHAPTER FOUR:
  Value Debate   83

CHAPTER FIVE:
  Policy Debate   104

CHAPTER SIX:
  Advanced Theory—a Deeper Understanding   163

CHAPTER SEVEN:
  Applied Argumentation   185

About the Authors   207

"Strong minds discuss ideas, average minds discuss events, weak minds discuss people."

—Socrates

CHAPTER ONE

Introduction to Argumentation

AN OVERVIEW

Lesson Objective:

Chapter One presents a very brief examination of the origins of rhetoric as well as the basic requirements to create a solid argument.

After completing this chapter a student should be able to:

1. Understand the origins of the art of persuasion

2. Grasp the distinct components of an argument

3. Recognize factors that affect the outcome of an argument

New Terms:

Empirical	Claim	Analysis	Pathos
Contingent	Argument	Impact	Ethos
Rhetoric	Backing	Logos	

A couple thousand years ago, rumor has it that a Greek rhetorician named Corax nearly at the end of his career, thought it prudent to assist the next generation with his knowledge. Thus he hung out a shingle indicating he was willing to offer his skills as an orator, should a willing student step forward. Tisias was such student and the two embarked on the dissemination of knowledge surrounding the art of words, today known as persuasion.

In exchange for the training, Tisias agreed to pay Corax a designated fee after he won his first case. After months if not years of rigorous tutelage, Tisias ventures forth on his own, able to use the learned skills as he saw fit. After a few years of not receiving payment, Corax became suspicious as to whether Tisias was holding out or had simply not had an opportunity to make his case in court. Either way, Corax called his bluff by bringing suit against Tisias to recover the fee for his services. The following is a nearly precise transcript of what the judges heard on that fateful day.

<u>Tisias</u>: Your Honors, I stand here today with a pure heart in awe of your knowledge, asking only that you listen and issue as fair of a verdict as you are capable.

    I charge that Corax failed to properly teach me the art of rhetoric, or persuasion…like I can't convince people with my words and stuff. The proof is here before us. If I lose my case, it proves my point that I was not taught well. And if that's the case, I should NOT have to pay his fee. No one should have to pay for services that weren't rendered according to what was promised.

On the other hand, if I win, it shows that I had enough knowledge and talent to figure out the art of rhetoric on my own, despite the inadequacies of my instructor. But even if that is not necessary to my case, a ruling against Corax is a ruling for me. And a ruling for me means I don't need to pay him. In either case, then, I should NOT be required to pay Corax one cent.

<u>Corax:</u> Your Honors, I, too, stand in awe of your knowledge. In my many years of speaking in front of you, I have learned of you fine decision making skills and know of your commitment to making decisions that serve justice. Thank you for taking the time to hear my complaint.

I have given Tisias the best education in rhetoric that I could muster, assuming that someday he would choose to pay me for my services. Yet, in looking through my check book, I see no deposits from Corax. If you rule against me – meaning Tisias wins the case – then that shows that I taught him well, meaning he needs to pay up. If, however, Tisias does not win his case, that would show him to be an intellectually deficient. Those of us with years of wisdom, know that faithful, honest, hardworking teachers cannot be blamed students that are simply too stupid or too lazy (or too both) to take advantage of the expertly rendered services.

But even if this is unnecessary to my case, a ruling against Tisias is a ruling in favor of me. Such a ruling would, of course, mean that Tisias must pay up. Thus, matter how you slice it, either way my fee should be paid.

The judges were perplexed, and after what seemed like minutes, yet may have only been seconds, the justices issued their decision "KAKOU KORAKOS KAKON OON." Which translates as "From a bad crow, comes a bad egg." Or, "When a mischievous bird of prey lays an egg, the egg too is mischievous." Not to pass up a chance for a laugh, the ever so renowned Greek sense of humor is shown when we translate the litigant's names and discover that the verdict was a play on words with Corax meaning "crow"; and Tisias meaning "eggs."

As it was determined that the case was not much for future TV, the case was, essentially, thrown out of court.

Aside from prompting closer scrutiny of eggs, the case of the first two legal rhetoricians teaches us a great deal about the way people reason, hence we learn what the first steps are in crafting an argument.

In general, an examination of conflicting issues prompts a twofold examination, to determine which of the following two fields the issue may lie.

Empirical (Apodictic)
- These questions can be solved by objective analysis.
- "Is the earth an oblate spheroid?"

Contingent
- This is the view of politics, law, religion, interpretive fields, etc.
- "Was Reagan a good president?"

- This is the domain of rhetoric

Corax and Tisias saw that when people make arguments, they are not so much concerned with what is true, as they are concerned with what is likely to be true, or what is probably true.

If a woman is accused of assaulting a man, we would think that she probably did not do it, since most of the time, women don't assault men.

They realized that knowledge is a construct of humans and that persuasion doesn't deal with certainty, only probability. And any judgments based on probability depend upon experience.

If we have had experience with a thing, then we can make judgments based on that experience.

The broader our experience, the more accurate our judgments based on probability.

Their discovery is still in play today, hence the continued utility and application of argumentation based on their early findings regarding rhetoric. Rhetoric, which they may have defined as the art of seeking capture, in opportune moments, what is appropriate and attempts to suggest what is possible, is in other words, a pleasant sounding arrangement of words with the common goal of winning an argument. With the ambiguity that is ever present in language, at the very least, it is incumbent upon us to protect ourselves from being flummoxed and have the opportunity to persuade in turn.

Corax and Tisias knew the power inherent in the arrangement of their words. They knew they needed to do more than simply win an argument. While a win would have sufficed regarding their day in court, it is true persuasion that we generally seek as a resolution to a dispute. Winning typically means another party is feeling the sting of a loss, motivating them to continue the fight, and possibly even seek revenge. Whereas persuasion offers the opportunity to have your position examined, evaluated and, if accepted, results in lasting change that typically gets you what you want.

The most effective form of persuasion stems from an argument, which is nothing more than a combination of statements (claim) which can be supported with proof (backing) , along with an explanation as to why the argument is of importance or significance (analysis), or has an effect (impact) on those involved (even if not explicit in the claim, backing or analysis).

Example

- Claim – Solar flares have been increasing in the past decade

- Backing – NASA has photographic and quantitative evidence measuring the frequency of solar activity over a given period of time

- Analysis – Evidence is unbiased, scientific and indisputable, showing proof of the heightened occurrence of solar flares in the last ten years

- Impact – Potential adverse health effects and/or disruptions in global communications may occur as a result of the solar radiation

Now that we grasp the basic structure of an argument, we should note that the effectiveness of a given argument is a matter of content and delivery, both of which are modified by the person making the argument. Over 2000 years ago, Aristotle recognized these 3 concepts (**logos, pathos, ethos**) which provide the bedrock of modern argumentation.

In examining a typical argument, there will be portions that are seemingly intuitive, meaning that it stands to reason. This would be a claim, supported by clearly defined backing, often of the scientific nature. Such an argument could be said to contain **logos**, or reasoning from a logical basis.

Anyone worth their salt, would probably claim that their argument is grounded in logic. However the best analysis would probably reveal that an argument grounded in logos would have a commonly held fact as the starting point or premise. Thus, the argument begins with what is commonly held and progresses from there. Often, logos would dictate that the progression of the argument is sequential, easy to follow for the listening and not jumping to any rushed conclusion.

Yet we are all aware of instances where we have acted as a result of an emotion. Thus it is wise to realize that emotions, or **pathos**, are also a useful tool to consider when constructing an argument. In such an instance, the backing for the claim would likely be anecdotal and highly inflammatory. While this may not be the most valued approach in argumentation, it is nonetheless effective on occasion.

Evaluating identical arguments delivered in radically different manners, should further illustrate pathos. Assume an argument is made regarding the physical dangers of riding a motorcycle without a helmet. Backed primarily with statistics, studies and cost benefit analysis, the argument may still be ignored by an audience. Whereas, if the argument were made by incorporating a heart wrenching narrative, examining the lingering side effects of losing a loved one in such a manner might be much more compelling depending on your personal preferences or experiences.

There are also times that the individual making the argument, or providing the backing to an argument is critical as to the effectiveness of the overall argument. We all have friends that are most reputable, with opinions that we value, but then again there are some issues on which we would not value their opinion. The overall credibility, integrity, honesty and trustworthiness of a given individual is knows as **ethos**, which may or may not cause the backing of a claim to be considered valid.

Examining identical arguments from 2 distinct sources might further illuminate the concept of ethos. Assume a close friend and total stranger are making the same argument. How will the source effect your perception of the message? Clearly, you friend has established a prior relationship, one that has probably been based on mutual trust, built up over time. The 2 of you have had many shared experiences, all of which have shaped your overall perception of one another. The stranger however, is an unknown entity, perhaps trustworthy or unreliable, yet neither would be known to you. As a result, we would most often follow the suggestion of the individual with whom we share characteristics, our friends. Thus, despite valid or invalid content of the message, sound or unsound methods of delivery, the ethos of the source plays a significant role in determining whether the message will or will not be accepted.

Determining whether logos, pathos, or ethos is most important is difficult at best. What may be more important is to understand the integrated relationship amongst them. Any persuasive argument will demonstrate and awareness of the interplay of all three.

In summary, an effective argument needs to ask and answer each of the following questions:

1. Is the issue at hand empirical or contingent?
2. Is the issue clearly articulated as a specific claim?
3. Is backing provided that is consistent with the claim?
4. Is analysis provided to establish a clear connection between the backing and the claim?
5. Is a specific impact provided, resulting from the claim being proven true?
6. Can the claim, backing, analysis or impact be altered as a result of logos, pathos or ethos?

CHAPTER TWO

Basic Argument Theory

New Terms:

Rhetoric	Rhetoricians	Dialectic	Toulmin
Model	New Rhetoric	Ethos	Pathos
Logos	Argument	Reason	Evidence
Claim	Argumentation	Ground	Warrant
Backing	Persuasion	Endoxa	Probable
Truth	Dissoi Logoi	Advocacy	Inquiry
Sign	Model Qualifiers		

HISTORY & BACKGROUND

Argument and argumentation has been studied as far back as we have any historical evidence. It was certainly a component of the Greek academies ran by such famous philosophers and **rhetoricians** as Plato, Georgas, and Aristotle. From that time forward we have an abundance of writings discussing the various techniques of arguing as well as elaborate justifications for *argumentation as an art when used as a part of rhetoric.* When used outside the boundaries of rhetoric, it was argued that argumentation became **"*quackery.*"**

Rhetoric was defined in Chapter One as the process of discovering the best possible arrangement of words in order to establish the truth of an argument as <u>part of the effort to persuade</u>. Basically, rhetores came to call all communications *with the purpose of persuasion* rhetoric, and disciplines such as <u>*dialectic*</u>, <u>*argument*</u>, and <u>*persuasion*</u> as necessary tools to aid rhetoric.

Throughout the years, the terms have often been blended together to the point that it is sometimes difficult to distinguish between them. Aristotle believed that you could not separate *argument* from *persuasion*. It is equally true that you can't separate the *dialectic* from *argument*. All three are joined together by logos. Persuasion, argument, and the dialectic are different from each other, but each uses the other to be effective. Therefore, in order to fully understand argument, it will be necessary to be able to see all three tools as separate disciplines.

<u>Persuasion</u> as a part of rhetoric means to win over to belief or to a course of action. That is the purpose of rhetoric. Persuasion is the <u>*product*</u> of rhetoric in that it focuses on the decision making or outcome of the rhetoric. Persuasion uses argument as the foundation of that message. Argument and dialectic are the primary sources of *logos (logic)* for persuasion. *Pathos (emotion)* and *ethos (character)* are also an essential part of the equation. The process of persuasion takes all that and runs it through a lens of values and context as they relate to an audience.

The **_dialectic_**, on the other hand, focuses more on logos--issues and arguments, evidence and logical proofs. The dialectic does not directly address audiences, or emotions, or contexts. It is assumed that when something is logical, it will be accepted. It is often aligned with logic and philosophy, but it has always been a part of the study of rhetoric as well. A working definition of the **dialectic** is to overcome disbelief and objection by argument and/or evidence. To Aristotle, the **_dialectic_** was a series of questions and answers leading to **_exposing the "probable_."** It was an important part of logos. The philosophers thought it helped lead to the discovery of truth. Often it involved looking at an argument theoretically without the clutter of anecdotal evidence.

The **_dialectic_** employs the inventing of arguments for and against a proposition. Each argument starts from a basic premise (**endoxa**) that is believed to be true. Instead of emphasizing only the arguments for an issue, the dialectic also employs the idea of **_dissoi logoi,_ or** contradictory arguments. So, using the dialectic means finding all of the arguments for and against an argument.

Sometimes orators use this method to establish arguments that will "sell" their position. It doesn't always matter if the argument is true or not. Check your local politician for examples of this practice. This use of the dialectic has given the dialectic a bad reputation at times and is called sophistry. However, when used with a goal of discovering the truth, the dialectic provides necessary elements to the **_process_** of argumentation.

Throughout history, the **_dialectic_** and **_rhetoric_** have paralleled each other, and rhetores used the **_dialectic_** as part of the **_process_** to persuade. The reason seems logical as both have as their goal to win over an audience, one focuses on **_process_** using strictly the structure and establishment of argument (**dialectic**), and the other focuses on argument as a **_product_** through the use of *pathos* and *ethos* (**persuasion**). Logos is the thread that connects the two.

Defining Argument

Argument is found as part of both dialectic and persuasion. It actually provides the framework for both. The following figure may help to visualize how all three fit together under the heading of rhetoric.

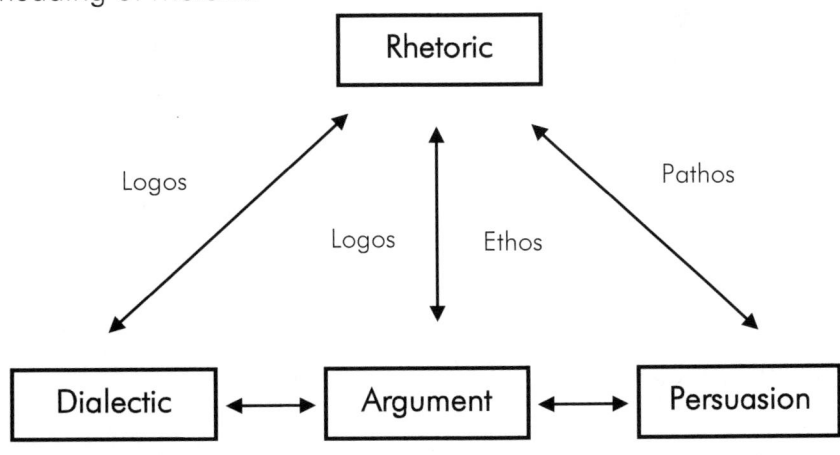

The term **_argument_** means different things to different people. Many people would describe **_argument_** simply as a disagreement. Using this definition, arguments break out constantly over almost anything. Simple questions like "where are we going to eat" or "where is my lap top" can be the cause of angry exchanges between people.

An **_argument_** for the purpose of our discussion implies more than just disagreement, more than a dispute or a fight. For our purposes, an **_argument_** starts with a _conclusion (claim)_. A person _concludes_, _asserts_, or _claims_ that something is true. However, just asserting something as true is useless unless it can be supported.

Therefore, the second part of an argument is to support the conclusion with **_reason_** _(warrant) and_ **_evidence_** _(ground, or data)_.

Reason means taking the claim to its logical conclusion. A person can do this through logical analysis or by using analogy, metaphor, or other figures of speech. Reasoning also is situational. What seems "at first glance" to be a solid unchanging issue can, within different parameters, seem entirely dissimilar from the first understanding of the issue.

At first glance, a securely employed person during a time of high employment might be inclined to claim that poverty was only a product of the lazy and disabled. A year later, after the employer filed for bankruptcy and closed the doors, that person might have more compassion for families needing government assistance.

This situational difference affects both the messenger and the audience.

Reason, therefore, must be accompanied by critical thought as to the *assertion* or *claim*, the context or situation, and the people making the claims. Reasoning may lead the claimant or the listener to question the original claim or presumptions. If that in fact happens, claims and presumptions could or should be modified.

Evidence is usually thought of as <u>data or facts</u>. That data could be either qualitative, which would include such facts as expert opinion and anecdotal examples, or quantitative, which would include such facts as empirical examples, and statistics.

Process or Product?

Quackery or Art? The above definition of argument gives us the basic elements by focusing on the **process,** but fails to address the situational nature and the intended consequences from the argument. Remember that the definition of rhetoric is communications with the purpose of persuasion. It is rhetoric that is an art.

As we said above, argument is a big part of persuasion, which is the purpose of rhetoric. It is important to see the connection. It is the analysis of the **product** of an argument and its consequences that transforms the argument into the field of rhetoric and makes it an art.

The consequence of an argument is the **product** of the argument, and the **product** of an argument is its effect upon an audience.

Argument is used both formally and informally. Audiences in formal argument can be quite different than audiences of informal argument. In formal argument, the **_process_** is used to demonstrate absolute truth.

We run all the evidence through a logical **process** to arrive at the truth. Formal arguments are found in science, math, and legal proceedings.

In informal argument that absoluteness is not possible. *Who is the greatest baseball player?* Adequate evidence exists to support several conclusions to that question. Without definitive proof, opinion enters the discussion and the audience determines the validity of the evidence.

The purpose is not to find the absolute truth but the most probable truth. In the study of informal argument, the **_product_** then becomes the focus.

As was said earlier, it is impossible to separate argument from persuasion or argument from the dialectic. They are separate disciplines and can be studied independently, but effective rhetoric blend the use of all three.

The diagram that followings further indicates how all the elements we have been discussing fit together.

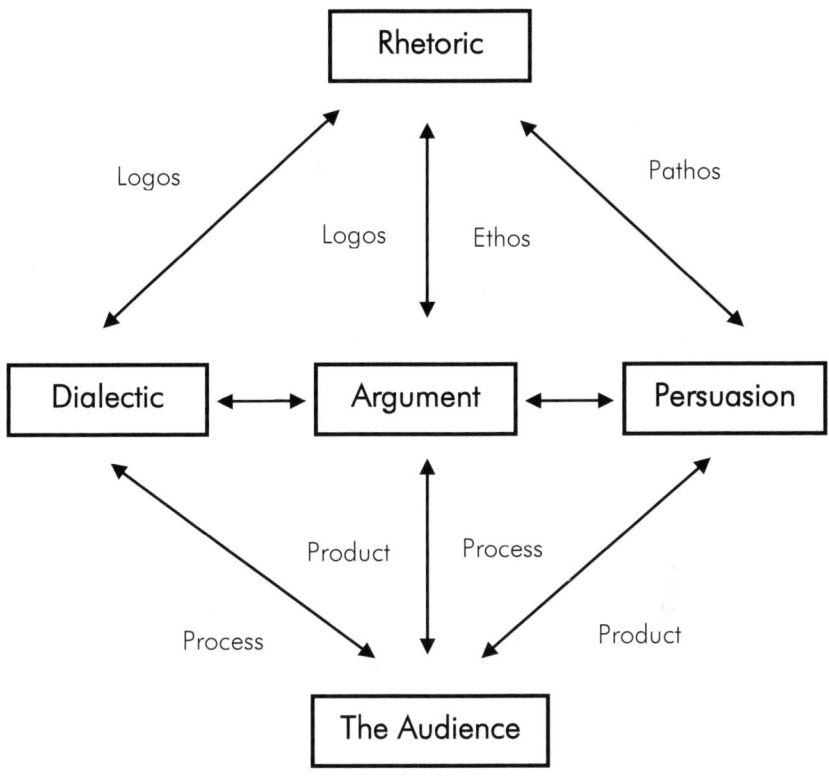

When that focus centers on the *product* and how it would affect an audience, the argument becomes a part of **persuasion** and is what Aristotle suggests makes Rhetoric an "art."

To help you further understand the relationships that exist between the dialectic, argument, and persuasion, it might be helpful to turn the diagram above up-side-down and start with the audience. This was the approach suggested by Chaïm Perelman when he looked at argument.

Perelman thought that argument should be looked at through the eyes of an audience *(product)*. This caused Perelman to look at evidence in a different way from other experts. He thought that each audience came with different experiences, education, and values. He grouped facts, truths and presumptions under the heading of _reality_. Reality, like reason, is situational. What is reality to one person is not necessarily reality to another. Evidence to Perelman is what is considered "real" to an audience.

In my community, reality is that it is safe to walk alone at night. There is little traffic and I know all my neighbors. Facts would say that there has never been a criminal act of violence ever in my neighborhood. That is my reality. Someone who lives in another place might have different facts and thus a different reality.

ETHICS & RESPONSIBILITIES

Before we go any further, it should be helpful to look at our other definition. **Argumentation** usually means the use of an argument. However, for our purposes we will add two requirements to that use. First, argumentation implies that the argument will be made to someone. Either written or presented orally, _argumentation implies an audience._ Second, a purpose is implied. Unlike an argument with a sister or a brother, the purpose is not just to irritate someone. Argumentation implies that the argument is to be used as part of an effort to get to the truth of the conclusion being argued. _Argumentation is the search for the probable truth._

Unlike some authors who claim that the goal of argumentation is only to gain assent or agreement, the authors here will maintain that argumentation in everyday discourse is a way for participants to establish reasonable or probable truth. When referring to probable, it is not in the context of calculable probability. The reality in the "real world" is that our truth is not very often absolute. Truth is more a result of opinion. Those opinions are based upon reality and the things we prefer. Probable truth, then, becomes based upon justifiable opinion. This becomes our ethical base and our responsibility to the audience.

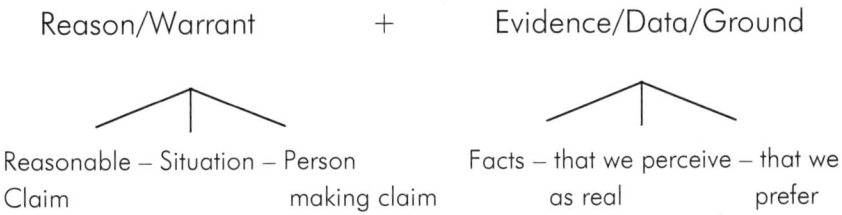

Reason/Warrant   +   Evidence/Data/Ground

Reasonable – Situation – Person   Facts – that we perceive – that we
Claim   making claim   as real   prefer

Equals Probable Truth

Where We Begin

Informal argument or every day argument is not simple and clean. It can be messy, but it is the type of argument that we all use the most. For that reason, the focus of this book will be more to that type of argumentation. With all this background understood, the best place to start a study of a basic argumentation theory is at the *"start."*

When making a claim or assertion to an audience, it is helpful to know points of agreement between the claimant and the audience. When a claim needs further support, the place to start is with the evidence or reality shared with the audience, not that with which they disagree. **These are often called starting points or shared or common ground.**

When making the claim that city government should pass ordinances that prohibit smoking in restaurants, it was necessary that to start the argument with factual points of agreement such as smoking causes cancer and that second hand smoke can also cause cancer.

After agreement is reached on those points, the issues in contention take on a different level of importance and hierarchies can be established.

Chaim Perelman breaks these points of agreement into two groups: *that we perceive as real*, which we just discussed, and *that which we prefer*, such as values and hierarchies. In everyday argument, it is just important to consider the audience's attitude toward evidence as it is for that evidence to be true. This corresponds to the reason part of the definition presented above.

Overview

In the first chapter, an argument that took place a long time ago between Corax and Tisias was offered as a framework for a discussion of the elements that make up an argument. Once those elements were discovered, it was then possible to evaluate the techniques used as to their effectiveness. It was discovered that certain techniques were more effective than others at persuading an audience of the probable truth of a claim. As was also mentioned in Chapter One, that whole process of discovering the best possible arrangement of words in order to establish the truth of an argument as part of the effort to persuade is called **rhetoric**.

In this chapter, argument, persuasion, and the dialectic were described as component parts of **rhetoric**. While the focus of this chapter is on argument, it is impossible to completely separate one from the other as they constantly interact with each other. Therefore, this discussion of argument will necessarily be also a discussion of persuasion and the dialectic as well. As we further examine argument with an **<u>emphasis on structure as well as function</u>** (*process as well as product*) in the realm of everyday argument, the dialectic and persuasion become important.

Structure

Classical rhetoricians like Aristotle and Cicero looked at arguments as both a process and as a means of examining a finished product. Classical rhetoricians were familiar with formal logic and treated arguments as if they were arguments offered in a court of law, made in a public forum, or as part of a scientific proof but still recognized the value of the outcome of an argument.

While structure was a key factor of the classical rhetorics, all rhetoricians recognized argument as a means to an end and provided elements like figures of speech that would provide support to an argument and help produce desired results.

It was, however, the 20th Century before rhetoricians started looking structurally at arguments as they actually happened in real life. It was then that a man named Stephen Toulmin began to look at every day arguments more as a *process* and less as a *product*. In this way Toulmin could identify the structure of the argument and identify the elements within every day arguments.

Many other people have throughout history proposed argument structures, and they all are useful for different purposes. This book will focus upon the **Toulmin Model** as it accurately describes <u>**the structural aspect of argument**</u> (*the process*) as it takes place informally in real life.

This will allow the reader a larger frame of reference from which to draw up examples and see relationships between the various elements of an argument. Further, Toulmin provides the best way to look at argument as a process of inference as well as the product of demonstration.

Function

The part of the **Toulmin Model** that we will focus upon identifies what is (*the process*). The assumption is that if the process is good, the product will be good also. This process borrows from the *dialectic*. It does little to tell us if what is being said (*the product*) actually had any effect (upon the *audience*). The Toulmin Model will help identify the elements of both good and bad arguments.

We will need to use different models to evaluate the effectiveness of the arguments. To do this we will need to identify the elements of persuasion. To look at an argument from a **persuasive** standpoint (*functional aspect of argument /the product*) and identify elements of effectiveness, it will be necessary to consider two different models.

As one of these models, this book will use Aristotle's persuasive proofs, his three appeals, **ethos**, **pathos**, and **logos** as the model that will help us identify the elements of persuasion. Normally, Aristotle's model is used to visualize the product and evaluate its effectiveness.

For our second model dealing with product of argument, this book will also employ Chaïm Perelman and Lucie Olbrechts-Tyteca's **"New Rhetoric"** as a rhetorical model needed for effective argument. Perelman and Olbrechts-Tyteca's model as well as Perelman's later writings emphasize the necessity of considering the audience when establishing elements of argument.

It is important to realize that the rhetorical goal of argumentation is persuasion. Persuasion occurs at three levels: cognitive, affective, and psychomotor. If an argument does not reach the cognitive (thinking) and affective (feeling) levels, the psychomotor level (*acting*) is less possible.

It is common for commercials on TV to appeal to our emotions (*affective*). People stirred to act (*psychomotor*). However, if a person is convinced at the affective level (*emotionally*) but not at the cognitive level (*thinking*), the lasting effects of the persuasion will not last once the emotions wear off.

Have you ever bought something from the internet only to be disappointed when it came? How many weight loss pills do you think a company could sell if all they listed were the ingredients (*cognitive*)?

Trying to convince someone to the psychomotor level (*actually doing something*) is extremely difficult void of emotion or data. Each supports the goal of the other.

What is being suggested here is that in order for the argument to reach all three levels, basic argument theory has to incorporate two separate disciplines mentioned earlier, **persuasion** and the **dialectic**. Persuasion focuses upon the ***functional aspect*** of argument, while the dialectic focuses upon the ***structural***.

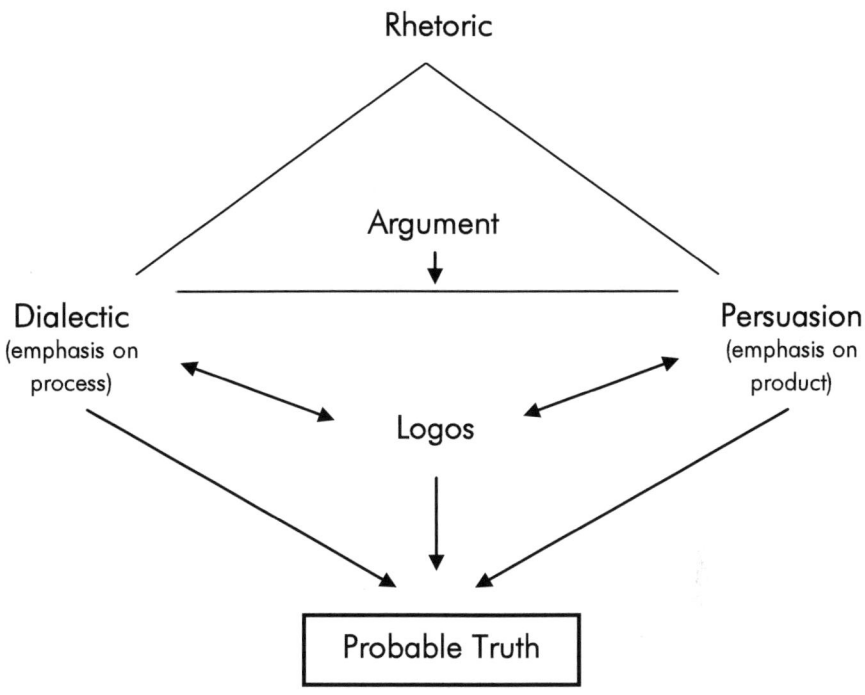

INFORMAL ARGUMENT—SOME CONSIDERATIONS

In every day conversations, much of our communication contains arguments in some form. Even when a story is told or information is given, arguments are usually being made.

However, when a person gives a personal opinion it might not necessarily be part of an argument. It may just be bloviating.

The key is intent. If the intent is to convince those listening, it becomes an argument.

The process of making an argument is to take information that both the speaker and those listening both agree upon (starting points) and apply those to assertions the speaker wants accepted. The goal is for the listeners to voluntarily just accept the assertion or claim.

If the listeners are not convinced initially, additional support is added by the speaker. This process often leads to further exchanges of comments and information.

Agreement comes only after all additional considerations of factual and logical importance to those listening are satisfied.

Sometimes justification of an argument may not be strong enough to be convincing. Consideration of this possibility is a question of product.

The reasons for failure to convince usually fall into two categories. Category one is that the argument was defective. Analyzing the process that was used may give an answer that the speaker may not have properly used all the elements available to the argument.

The second category is that the argument itself is not true as argued. When analyzing arguments, speakers should look at both categories.

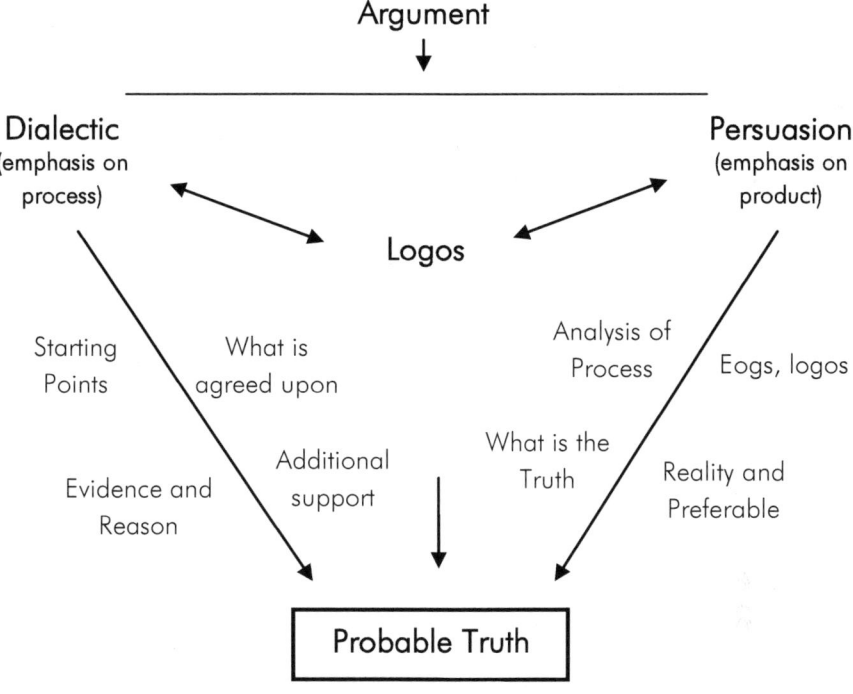

Arguments are also often divided according to goals. If the speaker is convinced of the truth of an argument and uses argument to convince others, the speaker is called an advocate and the goal of the argument is called advocacy.

If people, as they do on NCIS and CSI, use arguments to establish what the probable truth is, the goal of the argument is inquiry. This chapter will focus more upon the goal of advocacy.

>   Purpose to persuade .... Advocacy

>   Purpose to establish truth .... Inquiry

Up to this point in this chapter, several different words were used to describe the same thing. For instance, a claim was also called a conclusion, and an assertion. From this point on, we will narrow it down to one word for each idea.

The reason for the specific word choice is to eliminate confusion and to align with the literature that has been published. This produces more exact and precise understanding of each concept and points out a complex social interaction that exists within an argument.

THE TOULMIN MODEL

The first model we will look at in depth is the Toulmin model. This model allows us to use the dialectic approach to view argument as a process. Toulmin broke down informal argument into component parts.

He addresses arguments as "trains of reasoning," and he identifies the elements of any argument as (1) claims and discoveries, (2) grounds, (3) warrants and rules, and (4) backings.

#1) CLAIM

Arguments traditionally start with a thesis or point of view that a speaker or writer would want an audience to accept. Toulmin referred to this as a **_claim_**. More than simply stating an opinion, the clarity of the claim can be crucial to the clarity of the argument that follows.

Context and word choice in the statement of claim can either lead the way to the *starting points*, or provide a barrier to that path.

In the political arena, it is easy to find examples of this concept being poorly executed. During the last election, claims that one side "did not care about the poor," and that the other side "cared only about raising your taxes," preempted any chance at a legitimate discussion of the real issues. Instead, argument gave way to stubborn ideology, and the question of how to help the poor was never really addressed.

In our everyday discussions, our arguments often fall apart because of the ambiguous statement of the claim being discussed. Context and word choice are central to a clear argument in everyday discussion as well as discussions in court rooms, the legislature, and other serious debates.

Competitive debaters often say each word has meaning and that meaning usually depends on some kind of context. Regardless of the setting, it is important to start any argument with a clear and unambiguous statement of claim.

Parts of an Argument
Claim: *The assertion is clear and unambiguous.*

Claim

#2) Ground

Once the nature and significance of the claim has been established, the next step in an argument is for the *asserter* to establish the **grounds** upon which the claim is based. These are often what we refer to as "starting points' because the data and facts (evidence) presented are generally accepted as true.

Evidence establishing the ground in informal argument takes many different forms. In formal argument, the term data would be more appropriate than grounds as formal argument requires "hard facts" such as scientific experiments and statistics, along with historical facts, eyewitness testimony, and scholarly research. Formal arguments are more closely related to science, math, and legal matters.

Informal arguments deal with everything else. This is the kind of argumentation that we encounter every day. What will we have for dinner, should I take this job, and should I buy this house are questions that promote informal argument. The answers are not absolute. They can't be proved by science or math. Only the probable truth is the expected outcome, and that outcome might be different to different people. While the truth is not absolute, argumentation gets us as close to the truth as we can get.

It is in informal argument that the word **"grounds"** becomes a better word choice. The term **"grounds"** encompasses not only the data used in formal argument, but it also opens up a wide range of supporting information to support the claim. Testimonials from respected people, interpretations of actions and events, things an audience assumes is true, that which is considered "commonsense," and common held values and ethics are some other areas where supporting information can be as grounds.

Because informal argument deals with subjects that are difficult to quantify or to support absolutely, it is necessary that the supporting information for the claim (**grounds**) be unambiguous as possible.

Too often in every day argumentation, the arguments deteriorate when the grounds are weakly presented and become unclear. We all have heard the argument, "Yes it is, "No it isn't," repeated a thousand times. This happens when the grounds either are not clear or don't exist at all.

Validity of Grounds

In order for a claim that is in "question" to be accepted, it may be necessary to establish criteria for the validity of the "grounds." A second model can be used as that criteria. Aristotle's ethos, pathos, and logos are traditional examples of criteria that make the supporting information acceptable. 1. **Logos**: The grounds must be logical or have a balance of reason and fact. It shouldn't be counterintuitive. 2. **Ethos:** The grounds and the presenter must seem reliable and respectable. This would include the quality of sources, and the character of the presenter. 3. **Pathos:** the grounds should satisfy the emotions that the audience might have.

Usually a claim is made because of a problem. This evokes emotions from those exposed to the problem. It is necessary that the grounds provide assurance to the audience that those emotions will be relieved.

Criteria to assess the validity of the grounds could also come from the starting points we discussed earlier. The emphasis is on the acceptance of the grounds by the audience. Much of the contemporary research in this area was done by Chaim Perlman. He looked at the argument not as a process but as a product.

Starting points were discussed earlier in this chapter. For the purpose of supporting the claim, it is important that the grounds presented be a part of the reality of the audience. Either the audience already accepts the grounds, or the information presented as grounds for the claim should be easily acceptable. This establishes common ground between the claimant and the audience.

The Perelman Model also offers two criteria for evaluating the validity of the grounds presented: (1.) **That we perceive as real:** Opinions that express what is known to be true. **Facts, truths**, and **presumptions** constitute the "perceived reality." Perelman said that **facts and truths** were objective elements that "forced themselves upon everyone…" Perelman also believed that in informal argument, the audience's attitude toward facts and truths were equally important. If the audience did not accept a fact or truth, that fact or truth would not be counted as grounds.

Perelman said that **presumptions** are"…tied to common experience and common sense…" It is "… what normally happens and with what can be reasonably counted upon." (2.)
That which we prefer: Opinions that "express our preferences, such as our values and hierarchies, or which indicate what is preferable."

Grounds become the foundation upon which an argument rests. It is like a foundation for a house or a bridge. A weak foundation will eventually lead to the collapse of the bridge or house.

In informal argument it is important to establish a factual foundation with which an audience can accept, but it is also necessary to establish common ground with the audience for supporting information beyond data.

Parts of an Argument

Claim: *The assertion is clear and unambiguous.*

Claim

Grounds Data: *The facts or logical truths demonstrate the truth of the assertion.*

Grounds	Data

#3) Warrants

In Toulmin, Rieke, and Janik's book *An Introduction to Reasoning*, **warrants** were compared with a recipe for a cake. The cake is the claim. The grounds are the ingredients, and the warrant is the recipe that "combine those ingredients into the finished product," the claim. The warrant shows why the data/grounds justify the claim. In fact, the warrant justifies the audience's movement from grounds to claim as part of the persuasive process.

The warrant shows a kind of relationship between the claim and the data/grounds. Sometimes this relationship is omitted or stated briefly because it is clear and logical at a glance. Other times this relationship between claim and data/grounds is not so clear. In those cases, more effort will need to be made to answer the question of why are we justified in making the claim.

Parallel Comparison

In supporting the relationship between claim and data/grounds within the argument, the claimant can use **comparison** to assert that what is true in one situation is true in others. One type of comparison that helps support the warrant is a ***parallel comparison***. In this case, aspects of one must contain elements of the other, directly and explicitly.

For example, if Oklahoma University has successfully reduced its football scholarships and is still competitive, Texas should be able to do so with similar results. That same comparison could not be made with a Division II school because the elements involved are not the same or similar enough.

> **Claim:** We need to reduce athletic scholarships in Division I schools.
>
> **Data/Ground:** OU has reduced scholarships and are still competitive.
>
> **Warrant:** If it works for OU it will work for other division I schools.

Analogy

Another type of comparison comes from the use of **analogy**. In using an analogy, the comparison is indirect and implicit. While this type of comparison lacks the specificity of parallel comparisons, it is still useful in establishing a connection between the audience and the claim, especially when it is combined with other warrants.

Analogies can connect past experiences of the audience with what is being claimed. That can be good or bad. It is important that the similarity between the analogy and the claim be as close as possible.

> **Claim:** The gun owner is legally responsible for the accident.
>
> **Data/Grounds:** A 16 year old boy bought ammunition, went into his dad's closet to get a gun and accidently shot a friend.

Warrant: While there have not been examples exactly like this one, the court has consistently held that gun owners are responsible regardless of circumstances.

Generalization

Another way to support the relationship between claim and data/grounds is through **generalization**. What is true of one of a group or class is true of all. Sometimes the generalization is from some in the group to more in the group, while in other instances the generalization is from some to all.

If the generalization is to produce valid conclusions, certain requirements must be met. The **first requirement is that of class**. Samples within the generalization must be drawn from the same class or category and must be of the same class as the subject of the generalization. The old saying that you can't compare apples and oranges is very true.

A second requirement is that of random selection. Items used as evidence must also be typical. To accomplish this, a random sample is best. With modern computer technology this is a much easier task than in the past. If in a class of college students more seniors were used as part of the sample than freshmen, the results could be skewed.

Sufficient Size

Finally, the number of items used as evidence within a sample must be of **sufficient size as to warrant the conclusion**. When establishing conclusions about people within the United States, the statistics from one state would not be sufficient to warrant conclusions generalized to the entire population of the United States. This would be faulty reasoning and classified as a hasty generalization.

Connection

Instead of showing the relationship between the claim and its grounds by comparison or generalization is through the use of **connection.** **Connection** asserts that two phenomena are connected in a way that the existence of one infers the existence of the other. The two forms of connection are **cause and effect and sign**.

Cause

When arguing from **cause**, the argument moves along a time line. The first phenomena act as generative agent for the second. The argument starts with a causal generalization that is an If, then statement. If the cause is present, then the effect will happen.

> **Grounds**—Spring is causing a snow melt.
>
> **Warrant**—Melting snow causes rivers and streams to over flow their banks.
>
> **Claim**—Low level areas along these streams and rivers will flood

Some questions to use as test of cause are:

- Is the first responsible for the existence of the second, or does the one just happen to occur on after the other?

    Few actions are the result of a single factor.

    Look for "alternate causality."

- Is the cause capable of producing the effect?

    A cause must not only be *necessary*, but also *sufficient*. Oxygen is <u>necessary</u> for fire, but might not be the cause. Paper near a heater might not be *necessary*, but could be <u>sufficient</u> to cause the fire.

- Are other factors impeding or negating the cause?

    Conflicting or counteracting causes may be in effect. If a manufacturer buys more efficient machines at the same time wages and material costs go up, there might not be a reduction resulting in savings.

Sign

Another example of connection is reasoning from <u>*sign*</u>. Instead of the connection being cause and effect, it is symptom and condition. Reasoning from sign allows us to support our claims in more complex arguments where precision is needed.

Grounds: The Federal Reserve has been printing money to buy bad debt for the last six months.

Warrant: The Fed's policy has kept the stock market high and interest rates low.

Backing: The Federal Reserve indicates it will continue purchasing debt in the future.

Claim: Interest rates will not go up.

or

Grounds—Buds are forming on rose bushes.

Warrant—Rose bushes usually burst into bloom shortly after blooms appear.

Claim—We will have roses soon.

Some questions to use as test of sign are:

- How reliable is the sign?
- What degree of confidence do the sign merit?

    Certain indication of condition or action

    Possible or likelihood of condition or action

Reasoning based upon authority is a commonly used form of argument. The "if he/she says, it is true" is frequently used in commercials of all types. A problem of course is a failure to establish adequate foundation for authority. Qualifications of the authority need not only to be present, but said qualifications need to be relevant to the question at hand.

Other criteria to establish credible authority:

- Have access to data
- Authority identified explicitly
- Have education, experience, and training.
- Peer reviewed.
- Past performances
- Credentials are current
- Testimony from others of judgment

   Grounds—Dr. John Jones argues that salt has no negative health effects.

   Warrant—Dr. Jones conducted a controlled, 5 year, study of 2000 individuals.

   Backing—Dr. Jones received his PhD in nutrition from Kansas State University in 2002, has conducted seven highly acclaimed studies concerning dietary health, has written two textbooks about dietary concerns, and was recognized in 2012 by the Nutrition and Health Association as the association's researcher of the year.

Claim—The use of salt in any amount in food is a good thing.

Logical or scientific Warrants

Warrants fall into three basic categories. ***Logical or scientific warrants*** center on the logic of scientific reasoning.

Claim—The price of oil will go up.

Grounds—War has broken out in Middle East.

Warrant—War in Middle East has always caused an increase in oil prices.

Value Warrants

Warrants also center on ***values*** such as honor, integrity, altruism, and compassion. Perelman's Model would provide valuable criteria here.

Claim—Women should receive equal pay for equal work.

Grounds—Evidence shows women more productive than men.

Warrant—The constitution guarantees equal opportunity.

Artistic Appeals

Finally, Warrants can be based as emotional or artistic appeals. Aristotle's Model of ethos, pathos, and logos can provide valuable criteria in this situation.

> **Claim**—Asthetic bulletin boards enhance learning.

> **Grounds**—As a student I learned better in that type of environment.

> **Warrant**—Surveys of students showed similar results.

Parts of an Argument

<u>Claim</u>: *The assertion is clear and unambiguous.*

<u>Grounds Data</u>: *The facts or logical truths demonstrate the truth of the assertion.*

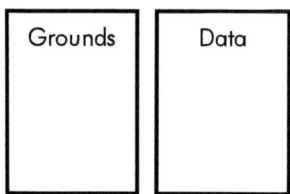

<u>Warrant</u>: *Assurance that the data are true establishing the validity and trustworthiness of the claim.*

#4) Backing

In some of the previous examples an extra element was added. It was labeled **_backing_**. Toulmin in 1984 said that *backing* was "...generalizations making explicit the body of experience relied on to establish the trustworthiness of the ways of arguing..."

In informal argument, ground often comes from sources that aren't as absolute as they are in formal argument. Warrants can appear narrow and overly focused. One and one doesn't always add up to two in the "real world." Backing provides clarity in these circumstances.

It is important to remember that warrants are not self-validating. The audience may question the warrant, especially if it is counter intuitive in any way. **Backing** simply validates the warrant. It reinforces the warrant.

Warrants must be reliable and relevant if the claim is to be believed. It may be necessary to put the warrant in a reliable or larger context and provide further documentation or additional information. Backing can contain evidence and should reflect the same logical, credible, and emotional focus found in warrants.

Parts of an Argument
Claim: *The assertion is clear and unambiguous.*

Claim

Grounds Data: *The facts or logical truths demonstrate the truth of the assertion.*

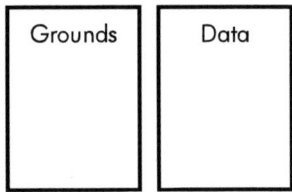

Warrant: *Assurance that the data are true establishing the validity and trustworthiness of the claim.*

Backing: *Assurance that the Warrant is sound.*

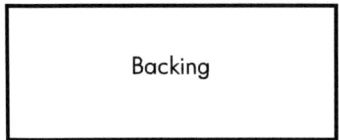

(Adapted from The Well Crafted Argument; White & Billings, 2005)

Train of Reasoning

Now that the elements are articulated, all arguments should be so constructed. Toulmin calls it a **train of reasoning** with each part linked to the others. When that linkage is established it may be said that it is a **sound** argument. Failure to establish one of the elements makes the argument **unsound**. The goal of course is to always make **sound** arguments.

Once an argument is established as sound, another question arises. How strong is it? Especially in informal argument, warrants seldom support the ground absolutely. In real life, the **"trains of reasoning"** are not 100% reliable. Practicality replaces the formality of demonstratable argument. Asserters of claims will limit or qualify the claim to reflect reliability through practicality.

Qualifications of an Argument

Qualification of an argument is obtained in four ways. *First*, *qualifying words and phrases* are used to reflect the degree of reliability intended. Necessarily, certainly, presumably, very Likely, very possibly, in all Probability, maybe, apparently, plausibly, or so it seems, so far as the evidence goes, and for all we can tell are examples of what Toulmin calls **model qualifiers**.

[Example of model qualifiers]

```
Backing    ┌─────────────────────────────┐
           │ As proven through time      │
           └─────────────┬───────────────┘
                         │
           ┌─────────────┴───────────────┐
Warrant    │ Aspirin and rest are effective in
           │ relieving symptoms.         │
           └─────────────┬───────────────┘
                         │
                         │      So, very likely    ┌──────────────┐
┌──────────────────────┐ │                         │ Taking some  │
│ Doug has a cold.     ├─┴─────────────────────────┤ aspirin will │
└──────────────────────┘                           │ help.        │
                           Grounds Qualifier Claim └──────────────┘
```

49

Second, conditions and exceptions are often expressed in real life argument in an effort to make the claim defensible. The claim is presumably true, normally the case, or very possible so. All conditions and assumptions are not always articulated. Rebuttals, then, become important as a means of identifying all exemptions and assumptions. (see example)

Third, sometimes decisions we have to make put us in a ***quandary***. Maybe we don't have enough information to make a decision, or maybe the information is conflicting. In either case, we often have to act anyway. It is a quandary. It is then reasonable to assume one particular position until the conflicts in the position have been resolved. Toulmin calls the lack of information and conflicting information **quandaries**.

Examples of conditions & exceptions

Backing: The black horse has been a good ranch horse for years.

Warrant: Ranch horses make good trail horses.

Jim says he is an experienced rider.

So, presumably (Qualifier)

Jim will ride the black horse.

Rebuttal

Jim will ride the black horse.

In practical everyday real life argument, we accept all kinds of presumptions. How do we know if our food is really safe? We have to assume innocence until guilt is proved in a court room. How do we know someone is really telling the truth? We accept things until there is a strong enough argument to prove it is not reasonable to accept it.

We also have opinions that we value. Opinions that have been passed down to us or we have learned through experience. We are entitled to those opinions until a strong enough argument is made to refute them.

Fourth, the **relevance** of arguments to their use provides some degree of qualification to the argument. The power or strength of an argument comes from its relevance to how it is used. Each element's **relevance** is tied to the other. For instance, if the warrant is irrelevant the claim would then be under suspicion of also being irrelevant.

In more formal argument, relevance can be established through more formal sources. A valid study, a survey, science, mathematics are aids to help shape the relevance of a particular claim.

However, in more informal argument we rely on common sense. Common sense is really a collection of experiences and understandings of how we act and speak in certain situations. This allows us to discern what exceptions we are allowed and what warrants are acceptable.

You promised to take your son to work with you. He is very disappointed.

Yes, but the boss sent me out of town. I couldn't take him with me.

Only knowledge and experience of both the boss and the father can give us an answer. That answer will include if the exception is accepted or not. Either answer could be correct for that person depending on the situation. Toulmin said, "...we are all members of a common "rational community," and so part of the jury by which soundness of argumentation is finally to be decided." Note that this decision of the relevance of an argument comes from looking at a combination of both process and product.

Summary and Conclusions

Our purpose has been to understand argument theoretically in order to understand it practically. Arguments are a large part of our conversation each day. We don't always recognize them, but they are there. Our ability to make good ethical arguments will determine the success of our relationships with others. This is just as true with informal situations as it is with formal experiences.

We first looked at a definition that implied that argument was more than a disagreement. We then looked at disciplines like persuasion, and the dialectic and their relationship to argument. We did not discover which came first, the chicken or the egg? We did discover that effective argument was interwoven with both disciplines and that all three disciplines operated under the heading of rhetoric.

To argue effectively, it is important for us to understand the parts or elements of an argument. These parts woven together produce a sound argument, but sound arguments can be weak. To give strength to our arguments it is necessary to establish the qualifications, possible exceptions and rebuttals, and relevance within the argument.

We looked at all this through the framework of three theory models. The Toulmin Model allowed us to see the elements of the argument (claim, grounds, warrant, and backing). It also helped us determine strength of argument by looking at the qualifiers associated with the argument. The Aristotelian Model of Appeals (logos, ethos, pathos) gave us criteria to help us weigh the effect of the argument upon the audience. Finally, the Perelman Model focused on the audience and how arguments were perceived by them. We discovered that facts and perceptions are seen by individuals as "reality" based upon their own experience. What is "real" to one, may not be "real" to another. Likewise, individuals look at evidence as "preferable" based on situation and experience.

What we have identified then, is that argument operates at many levels. This operative function exists on a continuum from the very informal argument to the very formal. As argument proceeds along this continuum, we must change our language and focus. Toulmin said that "...the language of formal "proof," "deduction," and "demonstration" takes over from the language of "support," "backing," and "establishment."

As we look critically at argument, we can conclude that we need to use one of two lenses. **First**, if we are dealing with formal argument, it will require deductive reasoning. Deductive reasoning allows us to prove the conclusion from within using the lens of process. **Second**, if the argument is informal or situational, we look through the lens of relevance (product). This lens allows for deductive reasoning, but also can incorporate the inductive or reasoning from example.

Finally, our examination of the term argumentation allowed us two perspectives that are important to *the use of argument*. **First**, we learned that argumentation always implies an audience. It is the audience that should determine the shape and form of an argument if persuasion is to be possible. **Second,** we learned that argumentation was the search for a probable truth. This establishes an ethical base for all who use arguments.

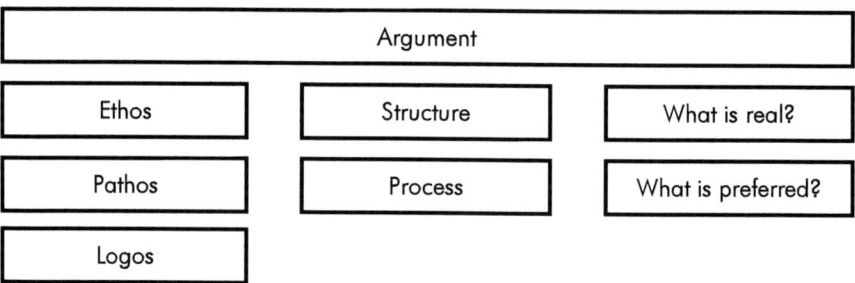

What we have then, when argument is looked at holistically, is a three legged stool as is pictured above. Argument is the stool and is supported by three legs. One leg is the process or structure. In identifying the process or structure, we used the Toulmin model to help us identify the various elements of an argument. Classical rhetoricians such as Aristotle identified the structure of an argument and recognized structure (process) as a key part of the dialectic and the center of formal argument. Toulmin's Model, however, allows us a better look at the structure (process) of informal argument.

The other two legs represent the product, and we used two different models to visualize the product in two different ways. One was through **Aristotle's Appeals**, ethos, pathos, and logos. Aristotle's Appeals are used in both formal and informal argument. These three aspects of the presentation are necessary for persuasion to be complete. The other model was **Perelman's** view of audience. Considering what the audience *"perceives as real"* and what it *"prefers"* allows us to shape informal arguments (product) so that they will be received favorably.

When rhetoric was defined in Chapter One as "that whole process of discovering the best possible arrangement of words in order to establish the truth of an argument as part of the effort to persuade," the words may have meant little. The purpose of this chapter was to dissect the theory of argumentation and show the close relationships that exist between the various elements of rhetoric.

It is hoped that exposing these relationships will allow the reader understanding and insight into using and evaluating arguments.

CHAPTER THREE

Fact Debate

EVIDENCE ANALYSIS

Lesson Objective:

Chapter Three presents a discussion of the elements within a fact debate as well as the techniques of evaluating evidence used to support arguments.

After completing this chapter a student should be able to:

1. Distinguish between a proposition and a resolution.

2. Identify the components of a factual debate.

3. Explain the role of the affirmative and negative in a debate.

4. Identify the types of evidence.

5. Evaluate the quality of evidence presented

6. Understand the difference between natural and artificial presumption.

7. Provide an reasonable resolutional analysis.

New Terms:

Proposition	Resolution	Proposition of Fact
Definitive Criteria	Cause & Effect	Impact
Core Issues	Basic Clash	Burdon of Proof
Prima Facie	Bias	Expertise
Consistency	Reliability	Relevancy
Validity	Sufficiency	Recency
Secondary	Enthymatic	Direct
Primary	Advocacy	Inquiry
Artificial Presumption	Natural Presumption	

PROPOSITIONS

Arguments do not operate just in a vacuum. Much of the discussion in Chapter Two was in the abstract. It centered on possibilities and theories to apply to those possibilities. An effort was made to find concrete examples, but the reader will only understand when the theory presented is used. The previous chapter focused mainly on argument and argumentation.

The next three chapters will examine argumentation associated with specific formats of debate that form the framework for discussion of the issues. That is why this book has argumentation and debate as part of its title.

Argumentation, if based upon a search for the probable truth will lead to discovery and solutions to problems. Forensic medicine uses argumentation to find time of death, means of death, and possible suspects. Science uses argumentation to establish scientific conclusions through research, study, and observation. Our courts use argumentation to establish guilt and innocence.

Argumentation is used in many different fields and in many different ways. Argumentation usually starts when an unanswered question enters a discussion.

In informal argument, that could be as simple as how are we going to pay for a new car or who has the best football team. In more formal argument the question is more thought out and calculated. In both formal and informal argument, the question forms what is called a **proposition**.

A **proposition** forms the framework for argumentation and is of three types: proposition of fact, proposition of value, and proposition of policy.

Each proposition focuses the argumentation on questions of fact, value, or policy. Answering the question that the proposition queries involves discussing the issues involved through argumentation.

The answers become the truth of the discussion.

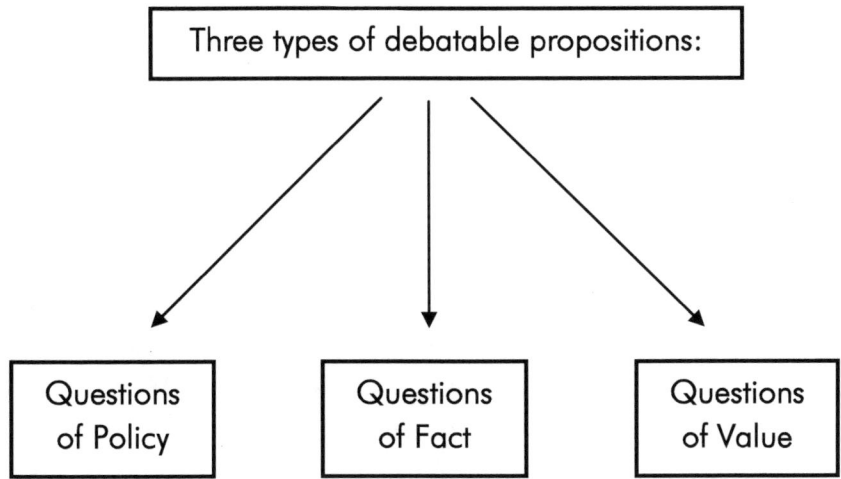

A proposition may form the framework of a scientific study and the argumentation produces just one answer. Another proposition may cause the articulation of all the arguments, and the answer may eventually clear up misunderstanding or provide the direction to problem solving.

It is also possible for a proposition to expose conflicting interpretations where truth can only be probable. It is this type of proposition that makes it possible to debate. This chapter focuses on propositions of fact and the principles of debating facts. The propositions used in a debate of fact should not lead to an absolute truth but to a probable truth.

Moving from Proposition to Resolution

It is the function of this book to place argumentation and the theory surrounding it into a debate format. This allows us to see and use the abstract in a more concrete setting. To be debatable, a proposition must have two opposing sides. These conflicting interpretations allow us to articulate arguments on both sides and eventually make judgments based on the truth exposed.

To accommodate debate, the proposition must be changed from a question to a statement in order to expose two conflicting interpretations of the facts. To do this, the proposition is made into a statement in the form of a **resolution**.

Example: *Proposition*: Is physical force a justifiable method of punishing children? *Resolution*: Spanking is a justifiable method of punishing children.

A resolution of fact should have a fact that is in question (justifiable method of punishing children), and a consequence of the action, (spanking).

Resolution = questionable fact + consequence of action

This produces a position of advocacy upon which a debater can defending a particular side. In factual debate, some of that advocacy can be replaced with inquiry. The focus can switch from I am right and you are wrong to a search for truth.

However, inquiry is more the role of college lectures and student term papers which simply answer a question. Debate, on the other hand, will force the participants into a marriage of advocacy and inquiry.

The Nature of Fact Debate

In a General Speech Class, it is usually taught that there are three uses of communication, informative, persuasive, and ceremonial. Argumentation as a part of rhetoric is also a part of persuasion. Propositions of fact tend to be more informative and less persuasive, but when the question becomes a statement, sides are formed and persuasion becomes more important.

It is your first day of high school, with all the hubbub of finding your locker, making it to your first hour class on time, meeting your classmates and finding out when you have lunch. You finally get through all the chaos and make it to study hall for the last hour of the day, thinking you should be in the clear, when the kid next to you starts in about your car.

"My car is much faster than yours!"

You reply with a winning shot, "Well at least my car isn't yellow."

The response pacts a wallop, "Your car is at least 10 years old."

But fortunately, you have an ace up your sleeve, "Huh uhh!"

"Uhh huh!"

"Huh uhh!"

Which brings us to where we are today. How in the world can we declare a winner of this debate, with so many valid arguments being made? The answer to that question might be simpler than you would think, and it is the focus of our discussion in this chapter.

The previous scenario is not unusual. It plays itself out countless times, whether in our everyday banter, our work situations, or even a courtroom. Claims are typically backed by facts that often come into conflict with one another, and these arguments revolve around the major issues.

This is the very nature of fact debate. If there is truth on both sides, it is debatable.

THE ISSUES INVOLVED

A resolution of fact can be divided into actor and fact. Once you decide the actor and the fact, the issues become clearer. In the proposition, "Natural weather cycles cause climate change," The actor is climate change, and the fact is natural weather cycles. Climate change is the fact and natural weather cycles are the actors. What is in dispute is that the actor, natural weather cycles, caused the fact, climate change.

Three **core issues** are involved in debate of fact. The first, **definitive criteria** (Matlon, 1988), involves defining the fact being justified with the goal of establishing criteria to justify the fact. In the proposition, "Natural weather cycles cause climate change," the core issue, definitive criteria, would involve defining climate change. From that definition, it would be possible to identify periods of climate.

The thought process would be:

> Identify averages of temperature, moisture, and weather patterns that are consistent over time. Change in climate could then be identified by major changes in the averages of the specific data collected.

The second **core issue** is **cause & effect**. Cause & effect involves establishing the consequence or effect of the actor's actions. In the proposition, "Natural weather cycles (actor) cause climate change (fact)," the core issue cause & effect would identify results from natural weather cycles.

The thought process would be:

> When temperature and moisture correspond with certain weather patterns, it is possible to identify the climate pattern as one of warming or cooling. If those periods of warming and cooling correlated with natural weather cycles, the resolution could be said to be true.

The third **core issue** is impact. Impact is significance of the effect. It explains the importance of the original claim.

The thought process would be:

> If warming and cooling were natural consequences, then the dollars spent and the opportunity costs that currently exist in our existing laws and regulations are huge. With the use of the resources lost, our budget

could have been balanced and unemployment could have been eliminated.

The core issues form three contentions which prove the resolution to be true. Each contention has arguments that constitute support for the contention. For example, the contention that the actor, natural weather cycles, causes (cause & effect) has several possible arguments. The fact that weather is cyclical and that it is the primary cause are two. Human caused global warming as a central focus of government policy is another.

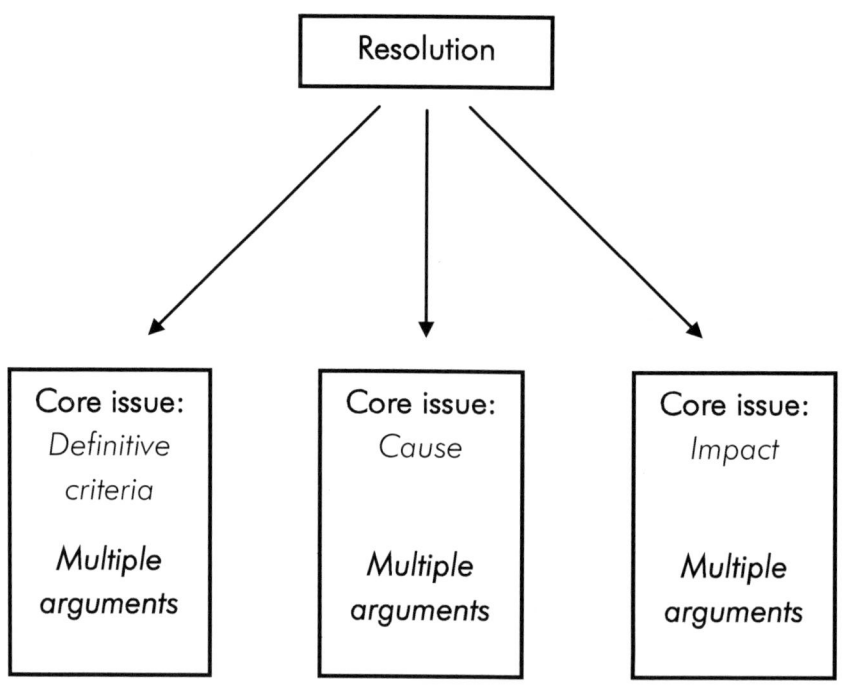

Affirmative/Negative

For a debate to occur, there must be two sides. Those two sides are **negative** and **affirmative**. The **affirmative** side is so named because it is the side that affirms or is in support of the resolution. All the examples above are from the affirmative perspective. The **negative** side is against the resolution.

The negative side, in the case of the resolution above, would say that humans, not natural weather cycles (the actor) cause climate change (the fact) resulting in global warming. Much of the argumentation would center on the issue of cause and effect. Possible arguments would be that humans are a more consistent producer of change, and that elevated rates of carbon dioxide in the atmosphere produce global warming.

Example:

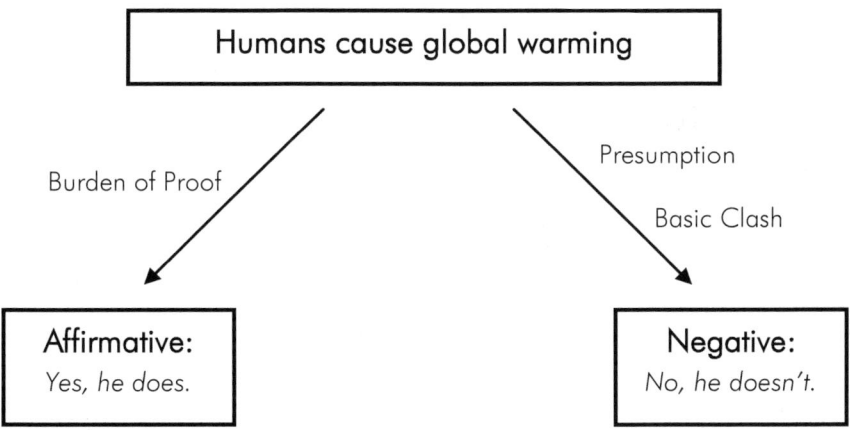

In a debate the negative has **presumption**. That means that if the affirmative fails to prove its case, the resolution fails as it was not supported. The affirmative then has what is called the **burden of proof**. The affirmative must prove that the resolution is true in the very first affirmative speech.

Presumption in a debate of fact must be either natural or artificial (O'Neill, Laycock, and Leighton, 1917). **Natural presumption** would go to the side that most of the audience would believe to be more apt to be true. The resolution above is worded according to natural presumption. Far more people believe that humans causes global warming and not natural weather cycles.

Artificial presumption is more concerned with the process than with the beliefs of the audience. In court case a person is innocent until proven guilty (artificial presumption). Courts are not interested in whether the majority of people believe a person is innocent or guilty. They ask jurors only to keep an open mind. Artificial presumption works well for the justice system, but it is less preferable for debates of fact.

However, it is impossible to know how every audience feels about a particular question, so sometimes artificial presumption is all that is available.

If the resolution above were restated as "Humans cause global warming," it would require artificial presumption. Most people today would be for the resolution before the debate starts. Technically the presumption would still rest with the negative. However, the audience or judge would probably vote affirmative if the debate were even. Negatives would practically have the burden to prove man did not cause global warming. Actual presumption would lie with the affirmative.

In court cases, juries are selected according to their ability to grant presumption to the defense and are instructed that a person is innocent until proven guilty (presumption). In debate, however, the audience is not usually select with such criteria. Many times it is difficult to obtain judges at all. Therefore, artificial presumption can place more burden on the negative than was intended.

Burden of proof is a burden of the affirmative and implies that the affirmative must prove the resolution to be true in the first speech before any negative argument. That is called **prima facie** which means that at first glance the affirmative must prove its case to the point that a reasonable person would consider it probably true.

This does not mean that the negative does not have to prove anything. Everyone operates from the principle of *"they who assert must prove."* Both negative and affirmative must support their claims. Remember the argument structure.

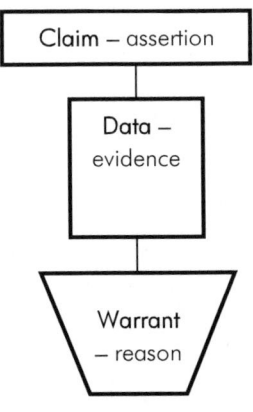

To be prima facie in the first affirmative speech and meet their burden of proof, the affirmative should provide enough argumentation to establish the core issues. Using definitions, the affirmative needs to establish criteria that will justify the fact. Then the affirmative should establish the cause and effect of fact, before finally impacting the effect.

Failure to establish the core issues would mean that, without evidence, the negative would win the round because of presumption.

Note: If the judge or audience believes the affirmative to be true prior to the debate, the affirmative would not have to work nearly as hard to establish their case. The negative, on the other hand, would have to establish a lot more facts for the judge to vote against the affirmative. Therefore, it is important for negatives to notice where presumption actually resides.

If presumption is with the negative and if the affirmative meets its burden of proof, the negative would then have to meet the affirmative head on.

This is called **basic clash** and is a negative burden. To provide basic clash, the affirmative must clash with at least one of the core issues. Negative could make arguments that disagree with the definition and criteria, that challenge the cause and effect, or that reject the impacts of the effects. Throughout the debate, both negative and affirmative present facts and analysis through argumentation that establish or deny the core issues.

Evaluating the Facts

Assume for a moment, the oft pondered question, "What is the best type of pizza?" With one side making a claim for pepperoni and the other side making a pitch for mushrooms, the battle wages, discussing issues of calories, saltiness, aftertaste, and cost. The list of reasons or facts supporting each side grows longer and longer, in what would seem to be a race to the bottom, with both parties attempting to simply offer more facts than their counterpart.

On occasions such as this, the largest number of facts would seem to be making the best claim. Yet upon closer examination, this might not be the case. We would need to decipher the quality of the claims, the manner in which the information was obtained, who performed the research, and more of the same.

Ultimately, a discussion as to which set of "facts" won cannot be reached until we move beyond a superficial examination of the facts and determine a criterion for evaluating the myriad of facts.

Audience Reality & Facts

Before establishing possible criteria for evaluation of facts, it would be good to remember argumentation theorist Chaim Perelman's viewpoint as was established in Chapter Two. Perelman lumped fact, truth, and perception together under the heading of reality.

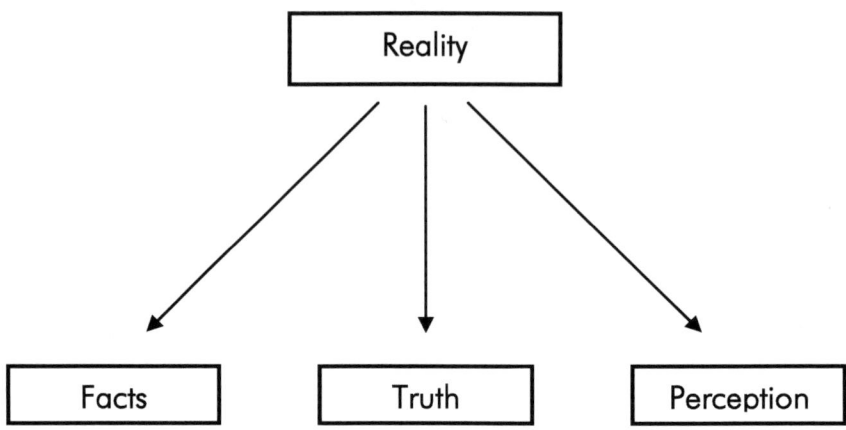

He claimed audiences brought different experiences, education, and values with them. Therefore, what would be real to one person might not be real to another. Evidence supporting a claim might be considered "real" and accepted by some and not by others, making it challenging to determine whether the arguments made regarding the best type of pizza were actually evaluated, or whether those involved in the discussion had a preconceived notion of what they liked best.

THE QUALITY OF EVIDENCE—EVIDENCE TESTS

One of the most common approaches to evaluating factual arguments would be to take a look at the evidence contained therein. Generally, evidence can be divided into two classifications, fact and opinion as fact. As mentioned earlier, facts are thought of as things that people believe to be true either because they have experienced them or they regard them as having been truthfully reported by others who experienced them. Most often, we come to believe something as fact when we can verify if through our senses or if it is a part of a common experience between ourselves and the party that did the reporting. Factual evidence is usually presented in the form of numerical data (statistics) via a report or as a personal narrative of an account of an object or occurrence.

On occasion, an artifact, or a physical object might be used to provide a basis for an argument. For example, showing a smoking steering wheel from you Lamborghini, which was recently incinerated in a garage fire, could prove to be an effective manner of proving the claim that "Fires are destructive." As we are often more compelled by what we see as opposed to what we hear or read, the use of an artifact can be very effective.

Opinion as fact is typically someone's interpretation of the meaning of factual evidence. Opinions are a judgment about how something is to be understood and or evaluated. Opinion is frequently offered by those that may not have expertise regarding a specific topic.

Further analysis into the quality of evidence allows us to distinguish between the quality of claims being made. In other words, when conflicting claims are introduced, the following standards serve as criteria for evaluating claims.

> **Reliability.** Are the findings replicable, or has the source produced similar information/data previously? Can the findings be proven again, perhaps over a period of time or in divergent settings?

Expertise. Is the source considered knowledgeable, or is an expert in the field? Such an expert will often have accompanying academic credentials. One can become an expert either through academic achievement or by experience in a particular field.

Bias. On occasion, the source may have ulterior motives that would taint the evidence that was produced.

Consistency. An argument should be consistent both internally and externally. Internal consistency would mean that the findings remain in line with other research and/or findings from the same source. External consistency would mean that the claims fall in line with data from other sources, largely making similar claims without contradicting one another.

Recency. Is the evidence outdated? Recent evidence is not always superior, but often the more recent evidence is more applicable to the claim.

Relevancy. Does the evidence apply to the claim that was made? Evidence can be found that seems to bolster a claim, but upon closer examination, doesn't really apply. Does the source offer factual support for the claim or simply state conclusions?

Validity. Is the evidence intuitive, does it ring true with personal experience? If it doesn't, it is counter intuitive and will demand better evidence.

Sufficiency. The sample is large enough in quantity and sufficient enough in quality that generalizations can be made.

Types of Evidence

Primary. The source is an observer or expert. Credibility relies on the source's credentials.

Secondary. The source relies on others, often experts. This is argument by authority and credibility relies on the reliability of the source as well as the one being quoted.

Enthymatic. The speaker appeals to the audience experience and knowledge. Credibility depends upon audience analysis.

Direct. Visual evidence. Artifacts and other visual evidence.

It is important to know what type of evidence is being offered as each type has its own issues of credibility.

If a round of fact debate focuses entirely on factual clash, it might sound a great deal like two sides each offering a list of reasons (facts) that can be verified through testing or research. This often creates a tendency to count arguments and declare the winner to be the side with the largest number of arguments. This is why an astute debater would look to evaluate the **quality** of the arguments via the above referenced criteria.

Proposition/Resolution of Fact and Competitive Debate

The final look at the resolution/proposition of fact will focus on the importance of the resolution itself. This in-depth look should have benefit at two levels. First it should help with resolutional analysis. Debaters should be able to determine from the wording of the topic where the clash is located and where advocacy is possible. Second, anyone involved with writing debate resolutions should take to heart the information that follows.

Propositions of fact in competitive debate have been famous for one thing: producing poor debate. The reason is really quite simple. Facts are the substance of truth, and who can challenge a fact? Arguments are usually more plentiful in affirming the hypothesis than negating it.

Besides, many of the resolutions are centered on truisms that can be proven empirically. Debating this type of resolution usually deteriorates into haggles of who has the most evidence. The criteria used to determine an outcome is usually preponderance of evidence. The goal is the discovery of knowledge that will prove a hypothesis.

While argumentation of that nature is a significant part of court cases and scientific studies, it is not good for competitive debating. Competitive debate needs a debatable proposition that searches for the probable truth within a question containing more than one view of reality. A resolution should produce two fairly equal sides. Each side should have enough substance to produce good argumentation.

When using that analysis, propositions of fact really fall into two categories according to the goal of the proposition. The first goal would be that of **inquiry.** This category of proposition would involve a question of history or science that can be determined by an exhaustive search of the facts, in other words, the existence of facts that prove the claim. This would involve a search of the evidence even to the point of establishing a study. The result would be absolute and without competing analysis. The goal would be inquiry.

Research papers, studies, and legal proceedings all fall into that category and basically provide a format to test claims made by a proponent using objective verification of an objective claim. An objective claim is one made from an observable event or from measurable facts. The proponent starts with a hypothesis and then attempts to prove it with a preponderance of evidence.

This type of debate, while very useful in expanding knowledge as well as in the establishment of truth, does not provide the necessary elements for division of ground that provide the basis of argumentation in competitive debate.

The second goal would be that of **advocacy.** This category of proposition of fact becomes a resolution and involves the analysis of existing facts and reasoning when there is opposing analysis and the conclusion is not absolute. This category of resolution of fact calls for a judgment to be made. It requires advocacy for the opposing conclusions in order to establish a **"probable truth."**

Division of ground becomes more adequate for debate when the interpretation of the facts and how we use them are a part of the discussion. Measurable facts and observations of events that can answer the question do not provide good debate. Difference of opinion as to the conclusions drawn are necessary for good argumentation in a competitive debate. This forces a process that leads to legitimizing the evidence and reasoning presented by one side or the other and evaluating the opinions of the facts offered.

The debate that is produced by this category of resolution of fact has as its origin in formal argument as we discussed in Chapter 2. Two advocates proclaiming different truths with the intent of persuading an audience provide an excellent the framework for competitive debate.

The answer, then, to the problem with debating resolutions of fact is solved by choosing resolutions from the second category. Resolutions should provide adequate ground for both sides.

If there is ground for both sides, debating a resolution of fact can provide as much clash as any other format. A somewhat hidden benefit of debating facts is that all other formats contain fact.

Learning how to debate facts will be useful in all forms of debate.

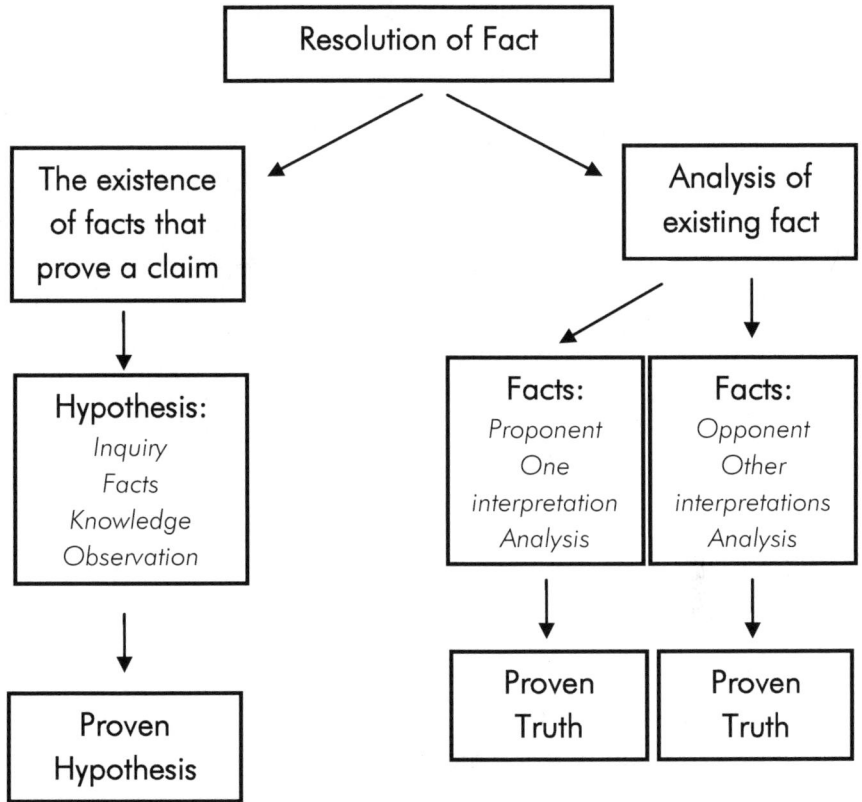

BURDEN OF PROOF & PRESUMPTION

Central to establishing negative and affirmative ground is the establishment of burden of proof and presumption. In policy debate, the burden of proof is directed to a plan of action that will solve a major problem. In factual debate, the issue is much less clear. Use natural presumption whenever possible.

The affirmative has the burden of proof in a debate of fact as it does in policy and value debate. The affirmative will support the resolution. Therefore it is necessary for the resolution to be worded so that it is clear where the burden of proof lies.

While resolutions of policy and value are worded to advocate a change in policy or opposing existing order, factual resolutions should advocate the most controversial side leaving the more popular side of the controversy (natural presumption) to the negative.

An example of a resolution in a debate of global warming would be: Resolved: Global warming is caused by natural phenomenon. The most controversial side of that debate would be that global warming is not man made and therefore has a natural presumption.

Stating the resolution as "Global warming is not caused by natural phenomenon," would cause problems for both sides. Since it is confusing to have a resolution stated in the negative, the first resolution provides the clearest division of ground. The second resolution is not only worded in the negative, but in a way that guarantees artificial presumption for the negative. The majority of the people would agree with the affirmative naturally.

Resolutional Analysis

This chapter has been dedicated to examining resolutions of fact. However, when debating any resolution, it will be necessary to first do some analysis of the resolution to determine type as well as identifying the core issues. We have discussed the core issues of a resolution of fact and will discuss the core issues of value and fact in Chapters Four and Five and that will provide the basis of core issue analysis within each resolution type.

When analyzing a resolution to determine its type, it is necessary to first look grammatically at it. It has long been recognized that the affirmative has the right to define terms. What has been forgotten by the new literature, and much of recent tradition, is that the word "term" does not mean all the words in the resolution. The word "terms" in this case actually means the nouns and modifiers in the resolution. The affirmative has the obligation to interpret the substance of the discussion. The nouns and modifiers included within the resolution create the possible actions, hierarchies, and/or outcomes of that resolution.

That does not mean that the negative cannot challenge the interpretations of the terms that the affirmative offers with a counter interpretation. However, the affirmative does have the "right" to establish a substantive framework from which the debate will operate, and the negative has the right to challenge.

The verbs, on the other hand, are not the property of the affirmative or the negative. The verbs belong to the framer of the resolution and are good guides in establishing direction. The framer has the "right" to choose the resolution type which provides direction to the core issues that will be debated. A discussion of "framers intent" within a debate should be limited to a discussion of the type of debate that is indicated by the verbs in the resolution. The framer gives up all "rights" to case areas and contentions.

The verbs typically indicate the direction to be taken. As a general rule, is, was, and are indicate a fact debate. Verbs such as prefer and choose usually indicate a value debate. Many times adverbs in combination with the verb help with the analysis.

Altogether, resolutional analysis in regard to debate type (direction) should rely on the verbs and analysis of the resolution as it relates to each framework type. (What exactly is the resolution asking us to decide?) However, not all resolutions fit nicely into one type or another. When differences in opinion exist, the affirmative has presumption in the matter. The negative has the prima facie burden of proof to establish their position. Close calls go to the affirmative.

Examples:

President Barack Obama is this generation's President Jimmy Carter

The verb "is" leads us to look at this resolution as a fact. The actor is President Obama. The fact is that he is comparable to President Carter. The results of President Obama's presidency define it and provide the criteria. The similarities of the two president's policies provide the cause and the results of the presidency are the effects. The impact would be the effects on our county and world. We are asked by the resolution to establish the fact that the two presidents impact the country and world the same.

In this instance, political assassination is a justifiable tool of foreign policy.

The verb "is" leads us to look at this resolution as a fact. Political assassination is the actor and a justifiable tool of foreign policy is the fact. Defining political assassination provides the criteria for what acts are involved.

The facts establishing a justifiable tool of foreign policy give us the cause and effect of the resolution. This resolution does leave a huge area of topic up to the debaters. "In this instance" is open to be defined by the affirmative. The negative can challenge affirmative's definition as too limiting or just wrong, but that is all debatable in round.

> *This House Believes that representative democracy is obsolete.*

Representative democracy is the actor. Obsolete is the fact. Since obsolete can be determined by fact and that is what this resolution is calling for, it becomes obvious that this is a resolution of fact.

As you can see, this is not an exact science, but hopefully these examples will help point the way. Try always to advocate or contest the resolution's truth and the debate will be worthwhile.

FINAL THOUGHTS

While arguments of a factual nature may be common in our daily discussions, they are rare in competitive debate settings, probably most notable within the confines of a larger policy debate or perhaps in parliamentary debate.

If a round of debate were to be focused entirely on a factual clash, it might sound a great deal like two sides each offering a list of reasons (facts) that can be verified through testing or research. This often creates a tendency to count arguments and declare the winner to be the side with the largest number of arguments. While all debate rounds have facts in them, debaters do not always argue facts well.

The principles put forth in this chapter relating to evaluating facts should be useful in debating facts where ever they are found. The reader is encouraged to challenge the evidence and the sources. Do not allow your opponent to use as evidence that which is not reliable or valuable in discovering truth.

An astute debater would look to evaluate the quality of the arguments via earlier referenced criteria.

CHAPTER FOUR
Value Debate

EVIDENCE ANALYSIS

Lesson Objective:
After completing this chapter a student should be able to:

1. Define the meaning of a value.

2. Explain how resolutions of value differ from resolutions of fact or policy.

3. Classify values according to value hierarchies, terminal vs. instrumental, and abstract vs. concrete.

4. Articulate some of the problems associated with using concrete values.

5. List a number of basic values that may be useful in debating.

6. Demonstrate how a value may be used as a criterion in a competitive debating context.

New Terms:

Value	Instrumental Values	Terminal Values
Criterion	Values as "Musical Notes"	Abstract Values
Desirability	Concrete Values	Value Hierarchies
Spheres of Argument	Proposition of Value	

ARGUMENTATION

Argumentation theorists have long recognized the existence of several types of claims or propositions that may be used in competitive debating. Propositions of fact require debaters to support claims associated with establishing the truth or falsity of a given assertion. "The Republican Party will maintain control of the U.S. Senate in the upcoming elections"[i] or "Suspect X murdered Victim Y on the evening of September 2nd" or "The United States Supreme Court will uphold the Constitutionality of the 'individual mandate'" are but three examples of this type of proposition.

Propositions of policy call upon the debater to establish the general desirability of a proposed course of action as specified within the context of the resolution for the debate. "The United States Federal Government should substantially increase its annual foreign aid budget" or "The United Nations should enact stricter sanctions upon Syria" or "The U.S. Department of Education should establish uniform standards for teacher tenure in secondary schools" would be common examples of resolutions of policy.

The third type of proposition is the **proposition of value**. Propositions of value call for the debater to make what Austin J. Freeley and David L. Steinberg call "an evaluative claim."[ii] In the realm of competitive debating, claims of value would include examples such as: "Partisan political rhetoric is harmful to the democratic process in the United States" or "On balance, social media is a beneficial means for raising awareness about global human rights abuses" or "When in conflict, security is more important than civil liberties."

Even a cursory glance at these examples tells us that value claims are distinct from either value or fact resolutions in several important respects. **First, value resolutions are generally oriented toward making evaluative claims about present conditions.** Fact resolutions tend to be either forward or backward-looking. The fact in question either did or did not happen or it likely will or will not happen given the ebb and flow of current events. Policy resolutions (as done in competitive debate) are almost exclusively forward-looking; they demand that debaters discuss the merits of the policy change either explicitly or implicitly provided for within the resolution under consideration. Claims of value call upon debaters to render a judgment about the goodness, badness, worth, beauty, or general level of importance ascribed to a given thing as it is under the present circumstances.

Second, resolutions of value are distinctive in that they demand that the debaters render such judgments by employing

commonly-held human values as the basis for judgment. In the previous examples the reader will observe that the values employed by the debater may be explicitly provided within the text of the resolution (e.g. security vs. civil liberties) or may be implicit as is the case when debating topics such as partisan rhetoric or social media.

Finally, resolutions of value are distinct from their fact or policy counterparts in that they lend themselves more readily to qualification. Again, in the examples of value resolutions specified above the reader will notice the use of qualifying phrases such as "on balance" and "when in conflict" which help define the parameters of the value under consideration.

Although some fact resolutions will constrain the resolution to a discussion of particular future or past events, such constraint does not permit the debater to supply a qualification in the way they can in the context of a value debate. Similarly, it is difficult for a policy debater to credibly claim that the merits of a proposed policy ought to be considered only under a heavily-qualified set of conditions.

Given these distinctive features, it is essential that students of argumentation and competitive debating acquaint themselves with resolutions of value and the use of values in argumentation in order to hone their skills and become better practitioners of their craft.

In order to facilitate our discussion, this chapter is divided into several parts. We will begin by discussing what human values are and consider their rhetorical utility in relation to competitive debating. Next, we will note how these values can be classified.

Finally, we will discuss a number of basic guidelines that successful competitive debaters will find useful the next time they find themselves engaged in a debate where value argumentation is involved.

WHAT ARE VALUES?

There is an old saying about conflict. The saying goes that great conflicts occur not when right faces wrong, but when two rights face each other. What could this possibly mean? We as human beings tend to act based upon what we believe to be right, good, appropriate, or simply expedient at a given time.

Even in a case when expediency might lead a person to do something morally censurable (such as cheating on an exam) one might defend his or her actions by saying that the professor graded a previous assignment too harshly and therefore, the act was done to restore some justice to the situation; the offense was only minimal at best and did not constitute a serious violation of ethics. (We do not recommend that you try this by the way—either cheating or this flimsy justification!)

On the other hand, one can argue (as we would) that such an act would be inherently dishonest (since the person who cheated was unlikely to come clean about it unless they were caught) and would in fact be unjust in the sense that the cheating provided the student in question with an unfair advantage over his or her classmates.

In this example we see values at work in everyday argumentation. **Values are broadly agreed-upon concepts that express and reflect moral, social, or political desirability.** In the previous example one sees that somebody on either side of the controversy could claim that their position was most consistent with the value of justice. (Again, though the task of the person trying to justify cheating on the basis of justice is going to be far more difficult.)

The person who condemns cheating does so because of the lying and dishonesty it fosters, thus there are value implications involved in both positions.

Examples of Common Values

Freedom	Equality	Justice
Courage	Responsibility	Loyalty
Happiness	Pleasure	Quality of Life
The Family	Individualism	Self Actualization

CLASSIFYING VALUES

When a debater begins to think about values and the roles that they play in debate, it is useful to start by thinking of several ways to classify values. We would posit that there are three ways of categorizing human values—according to their level of desirability as defined by a culturally-bound value hierarchy, their status as terminal or instrumental values, and whether the value(s) in question are concrete or abstract.

VALUE HIERARCHIES

Naturally, in order for a concept to be considered a value, there must be broad agreement about its **desirability. Desirability refers to the degree to which something is inherently pleasing, helpful, good, or beneficial.** Each of the examples in the table above may be thought of as a concept about which there is broad (though perhaps not universal) agreement upon the goodness, usefulness, or beneficial nature of the concept.

In the context of a debate, values are an important element of a variety of the claims, sub-claims, and counter-arguments that are advanced by both sides. This is certainly true in the case of a value resolution. However, we would further posit that, even when not explicitly stated, values are often integral to the formulation of a wide variety of arguments.

Consider the policy proposition referenced earlier in this chapter: "The United Nations should enact stricter sanctions upon Syria." The affirmative would advance a topical plan presumably designed to cause the Syrian regime to cease their violent and repressive policies towards dissenters within their own country. One should notice that the advantages accrued by such a plan would have much to do with the promotion of certain human values. Some of these would include: human life, equality, democracy, free expression and the like. Similarly, the negative might argue that such efforts would backfire and therefore put the lives of more pro-democracy protestors at risk.

Thus, the values of human life, freedom, justice, and perhaps others would be at stake in this situation. As is evident from this example, even the most technical policy-oriented debate has human values as the explicit or implicit bedrock of one's argumentation.

Clearly values are an important part of debate. This is so because values are such an important component of what humans believe to be desirable. But how do we determine the desirability of a value within the context of a resolution? This is where value hierarchies come into play. **A value hierarchy is an argument made by a debater about the relative desirability of a given value(s) in a given context at a given time.**

One of us was once coached by an outstanding teacher who had an inventive method of explaining value hierarchies. Values, he explained, were like notes on a piano. No one note on the piano is any more important than any other note—indeed it would be silly to suggest so. Context and the time are the determining factors. In some situations, (as dictated by the music that one is playing) one note is the correct one or the best available choice. Applied to a debate, a value hierarchy is the debater's attempt to explain the relative importance of a given value in a given situation. In the previously-referenced Syria resolution, the affirmative may articulate that their policy is advantageous because it fosters democracy.

The negative may counter that it does little good to foster democracy if too many human lives are sacrificed in the process. In this case, the negative is not arguing that democracy is unimportant, but that it is not the most important in this particular case. Associating values with hierarchies affords debaters a set of tools to argue that a particular value (or series of values) is more desirable than others at a given time.

One final important note about value hierarchies is necessary. Human values, as we have already discussed, do not exist within an individual frame, but are communal. Thus, they are bound within a given culture and cultural context. Defining the term "culture" is not a simple undertaking. Nevertheless for our purposes we will, Gamble and Gamble who define culture as "a system of knowledge, beliefs, values, customs, behaviors and artifacts that are acquired, shared & used by members during daily living."[iii]

As this definition suggests, the things we regard as important are shaped, to a very large extent, by the cultural environment in which we reside. The value of individualism is seen as having a high degree of relative importance in Western cultures but far less so in Eastern cultures because Eastern cultures tend to value collectivism more highly—particularly when individualism and collectivism may be in conflict.

The values that are attributed to the process of information sharing serve as another example of the notion that values and value hierarchies are heavily influenced by the cultural environments in which they operate. For instance, accessibility of information and a clear vocabulary are highly valued by the general public, yet groups of experts or specialists in a given area all too often forsake clarity and accessibility for the use of technical jargon. When using values and constructing value hierarchies debaters will want to learn as much as they can about the culture (and sub-cultural) environments in which they will be competing and adjust their argumentation accordingly.

TERMINAL VS. INSTRUMENTAL VALUES

Of course, different values are desirable for different reasons. The desirability of loyalty, for instance, stems from the fact that one who is loyal in an interpersonal relationship or in a professional context will not leave at the first sign of trouble. A loyal person will also not betray the company for his or her own personal gain.

However, loyalty, unlike pleasure or happiness, is not terribly satisfying as an end unto itself. As such, it is helpful to differentiate between **terminal and instrumental values.** Loyalty is therefore what Milton Rokeach calls an "instrumental value."[iv] Rokeach explains that some values (known as "terminal values") are useful in and for their own sakes, whereas others are deemed to be instrumental in the sense that they can help us accomplish more "terminal" tasks.

For instance, "freedom" is a terminal value—something useful and desirable for its own sake, but "courage" is an instrumental value because its primary worth is in attaining something else (such as freedom).

Consideration of whether a value is terminal or instrumental may be helpful to a debater who is seeking to draw distinctions between his or her position and that of his or her opponents. For instance, when debating "The integrity of U.S. elections is more important than the right of free speech as manifested in campaign contributions" we see a potentially useful application of the terminal vs. instrumental values classification.

The integrity of the electoral process is important, but so is free speech. How can such an impasse be resolved? One strategy available to the affirmative in this case would be to argue that, when it comes to campaign contributions in the electoral season, free speech is a great value, but it is instrumental at best to the terminal value of democracy.

If the affirmative can establish that limits upon campaign contributions are likely to enhance democracy, then we should give greater credence to the terminal value of democracy rather than the instrumental value of free speech. Of course, this is but one of any number of ways that the instrumental vs. terminal distinction could prove helpful in a debate.

Abstract vs. Concrete Values

Excuse me, but could you spare a cup of justice please? Of course there is good reason why we do not hear this very often—if ever. Values such as truth, free expression, justice, freedom, and the like are all, to a large degree, abstract. Specific tangible objects that symbolize important or meaningful ideals such as a nation's flag, a valuable sports car, an historic document, a piece of art, or the like may be considered concrete values.

At first glance, it may appear that competitive debates rarely involve such concrete items. This simply is not so. Propositions of policy and value routinely involve discussion of matters such as the U.S. Constitution or a specific provision (or even a specific sub-section or paragraph) of an important federal or state statute. Other policy or value debates might deal with a series of arguments based upon (or perhaps challenging) the Bible or some other religious text.

To the extent that these tangible items express and reflect moral, social, or political desirability they too are values and aspiring debaters should have at least some basic familiarity with them.

It is often said that, for speechwriters, it is preferable to use concrete language rather than abstract language. While this is true for good speechwriting, it is not necessarily true when it comes to debates involving values. There is nothing wrong with using a concrete value per se, yet debaters should realize beforehand that appealing to a value that is too specific can expose one's arguments to a number of vulnerabilities.

The most glaring of these is that concrete values are still quite symbolic and therefore lack the specificity that some arguers may want to claim. For instance, it is very difficult in a debate to say that "my position is consistent with the Bible." An opponent cross-examining this person might ask a series of difficult questions about that statement including: "There are more than 66 different books in the Bible, could you be a little more specific?" or "What about this passage which would seem to contradict your interpretation?" or "Which version of the Bible is your position consistent with—the Catholic scriptures, the King James Version, some other version?" or even "Why is the Bible the most authoritative religious text on this particular subject?"

One might encounter similar problems when using "the First Amendment" as a concrete value. "Which part of the First Amendment?" "What about the varying interpretations of the First Amendment?"

We are not arguing that one should never use a concrete value—far from it. Rather, that one should be quite careful to define one's concrete value in very specific terms. The explanation that is required is perhaps one reason to avoid too much overdependence upon concrete values, but it is sometimes necessary to engage such value arguments by looking closely at the text of the First Amendment for example.

Methods of Classifying Values
1. Value Hierarchies
2. Terminal vs. Instrumental
3. Concrete vs. Abstract

How are Values Used in Debate?

As we have seen in this chapter, values are a central component of argumentation because they reflect and celebrate concepts that large numbers of people within a given society believe to be important. But how are values used in debate? The remainder of this chapter will cover basic methods and strategies for using values in a competitive debate.

Of course, the type of strategy chosen will vary depending upon a number of factors. Among the most important of these variables is the actual format of debate in which the participants are engaged. As such, each of the general techniques below is discussed in the context in which it is most likely to occur.

Value(s) As a Premise for a Case

Sometimes a debater will wish to present a value (or values) and use it (or them) as a premise around which to write an entire case (set of arguments affirming or negating a particular side of a resolution). This type of argumentation occurs most frequently in high school Lincoln Douglas debate.

Simply stated, the debater will choose a value that most clearly reflects the essence of a given side of the resolution; then having chosen that value (they) will construct the remainder of the case either affirming or negating the resolution with the value, value premise, core value, or even a set of several values as the focal point of the case. Richard Edwards explains this situation in the following manner:

A value premise or core value is an ideal held by individuals, societies, governments, and so on that serves the highest goal to be protected, respected, maximized, advanced, or achieved.

This means that debaters choose a value that, in their opinions, best captures the essence of the resolution and provide a focus for argumentation.[v]

If one were debating the resolution: "Resolved: Liberty is more important than national security" it might be a simple matter of the affirmative extolling the virtues of liberty as being more desirable than national security when the two come into conflict and the negative arguing the opposite while establishing the appropriate counter-value of national security.

However, the affirmative debater may decide that, in the context of the American political system, liberty is only an instrumental value to the terminal value of quality of life and may therefore choose to use quality of life as their value premise. Likewise, the negative might decide that national security is merely instrumental to the establishment of a just society and, therefore, would establish justice as the negative value premise.

Sometimes two debaters will both use the same value premise. When this happens the debate revolves around which side of the resolution actually best promotes the value premise in question. In the "Liberty is more important than national security" example, both debaters might elect to offer quality of life or justice or democracy as the value premise.

In debates such as these it is important that the contest does not simply become a case of dueling values, but rather serves as an important discussion of how each of the opposing values has bearing upon the vital issues that are to be considered within the resolutional context.

Value(s) As a Criterion

An approach more commonly used by college debaters involves the use of a value as a criterion in a debate. A **criterion is a concept by which everything else in the debate should be evaluated**. When a debater establishes a criterion (or criteria if more than one), he or she is asking that the judge evaluate the debate in light of whatever philosophy, concept, or value is specified.

Not all criteria are necessarily values; some might be a philosophy, a theory, or an entire philosophical/political system. The following chart illustrates just a few of the possibilities available.

Shorthand Glossary of Selected Criteria

Utilitarianism: A set of philosophical principles arising from the work of eighteenth century philosophers Jeremy Bentham and John Stuart Mill. The basic idea behind utilitarianism is that acts are right or good in as much as they promote happiness and wrong in as much as they promote a lack of happiness. It is not enough to consider the impact of an act upon one person; an act must be evaluated in terms of the quantity of happiness it produces. This gives rise to the common description of the doctrine of utilitarianism as having to do with "the greatest happiness for the greatest number."

Exigence and Salience: Two different ideas that are often usefully paired together. Exigence refers to a situation that is urgent or has arisen as a result of something important being under threat. Salience refers to the idea that some things (such as the value of freedom or the delicate equilibrium of the Earth's environment) cannot be restored once they have been destroyed. Thus, exigence and salience as a criterion demands that the debate be evaluated according to what is the most important and what is most threatened in the context of the debate.

Net Benefits: A net benefits criterion assumes that (in a policy context) both the affirmative and the negative will be able to produce reasons why adopting the proposed policy (if affirmative) or rejecting the policy (if negative) would be beneficial. The net benefits criterion asks the critic to consider what is most beneficial in the policy context.

Cost/Benefit Analysis: Like net benefits, cost/benefit analysis assumes that there will be benefits to adoption or non-adoption of the plan. Cost/benefit is a slight twist on this concept in that it also presumes that there will be costs involved. Cost/benefit enables the affirmative, for instance, to dismiss certain negative arguments by arguing that their plan already anticipates some cost, but the benefits that will be yielded by implementation of the plan outweigh the costs.

Pragmatism: Although pragmatism represents a rather complicated set of philosophical positions and assumptions, it can be useful as a criterion in a debate. Pragmatism is the philosophical notion (that originated in the United States in the late nineteenth century) that (in all things) theory and practice should be not only linked together philosophically, but that theory should always inform practice. Applying pragmatism to a debate is not as complicated as it may seem. For instance, if one were to build a case for the negative on the resolution "Organized labor should be banned in the United States" one could say that while the opponent might have an idea that conforms to a certain political ideology, a policy decision based upon this premise would be bad and ineffective policy because the theory has not been sufficiently tested. Therefore, pragmatism would militate in favor of the negative.

Values (e.g. Justice, Equality, Education, etc): Values can also certainly serve as criteria in debates. If a debater uses the criteria of justice for instance, he or she may say something like: "I would request that you (the critic) evaluate the round on the basis of justice. For my purposes today I'd like to define justice in accordance with philosopher John Rawls whose theory of justice can be boiled down to the essence of 'justice as fundamental fairness.' Thus, when evaluating the two sides of this proposition, I would request that you weigh both sets of arguments asking yourself which of the two positions is most consistent with justice." This basic formulation of a judging criterion is an effective way of incorporating value argumentation into an educational debate setting.

VALUES AND EVIDENCE

Given the importance of values as they pertain to human motivations and desirability, we should not be surprised that values also have much to do with evidence. One cannot simply assert (that) "justice is the evidence that my argument is right"; however, one can call upon values as a way to challenge evidence or strengthen the appeal that a particular type of audience might have for an audience or a debate critic.

Broadly speaking, evidence can take three forms: examples (short stories or illustrations that support a position), statistics (numerical data), and testimony (opinions that support a position). Regardless of the form the evidence takes, there are three ways in which values can affect the evidence used within a debate **amplification of effect, cultural negation,** and **sphere definition.**

Values can cause the persuasive impact of a piece of evidence to be amplified. For instance, in a debate over health care policy, one side may call upon a story (testimony) about a patient who was denied a potentially-life-saving treatment because the insurance company refused to pay for the procedure. Implicit though it may be, (the fact that) most audiences and debate critics would value human life over corporate profits would powerfully amplify the impact of the evidence offered.

Values are also useful in that they can demonstrate that certain opinions or policy positions are (and perhaps ought to be) outside the realm of the values of a particular community. In public policy debates about the legality of same sex marriage, the extreme and often violent comments made by some opponents of same sex marriage may give a few Christians cause to at least reject the call for violence because it does not reflect the values of the faith tradition.

In this example, the debater using this evidence should take care not to argue that the extreme comments are not reflective of all who would oppose same sex marriage. Nevertheless, evidence such as this can lead to a cultural negation of a position. Other examples would include testimony, evidence which argued that wholesale discrimination against Japanese Americans and others during World War II was a violation of American values. Such examples are a powerful instance of values at work in the evidence we use to support arguments.

The values (either implicit or explicit) within evidence that is used can also help to define **spheres of argumentation**. Richard Rieke, Malcolm Sillars, and Tarla Peterson define spheres as "collections of people in the process of interacting upon and making critical decisions."[vi] Essentially a sphere is a community united by a common interest, similar terminologies, and, of course, similar values. What does this mean in practical terms for debate? Groups of scientists will of course value evidence that demonstrates reliance upon the scientific method, religiously-minded audiences and critics will be impressed by the appearance of religiously-oriented values in the evidence presented to them and so on.

In this way, the type of evidence you choose to use will help define the audience of people who will listen to it.

Conclusion

This chapter has outlined a number of important basics that will help a debater improve their basic value argumentation skills.

[i] Propositions of fact as debated in high school or intercollegiate debate often include either a predictive element—articulating that something will happen in the future or they may be oriented toward the past—establishing that a particular event occurred at a specified time or place.

[ii] Austin J. Freeley and David L. Steinberg, Argumentation and Debate: Critical Thinking for Reasoned Decision Making 12the Ed (Boston: Wadsworth, 2009) 58.

[iii] Teri Kwal Gamble and Michael Gamble, *Communication Works*, 7th *Ed* (Boston: McGraw-Hill, 2002), 35.

[iv] Milton Rokeach, *The Nature of Human Values* (San Francisco: Free Press, 1972), 28.

[v] Richard E. Edwards, *Competitive Debate: The Official Guide* (New York: Penguin Books, 2008), 154.

[vi] Richard D. Rieke, Malcolm O. Sillars, and Tarla Rai Peterson, *Argumentation and Critical Decision Making* 6th ed. (Boston: Person, 2005), 36.

CHAPTER FIVE
Policy Debate

THE NUTS AND BOLTS: AN OVERVIEW ANALYSIS

Lesson Objective:

This chapter presents the basic structure of a debate and explains the basic role of each side in a debate. After completing this chapter a student should be able to:

1. Define what a debate is.

2. Explain the basic role of the affirmative and negative in a debate.

3. List the speaking order and the times of each speech.

4. Outline the basic components of an argument.

5. Understand what a policy debate is.

6. Identify the basic issues.

New Terms:

Debate	Proposition of Policy	Justification
Affirmative	Basic Clash	Status Quo
Negative	Resolution	Change
Probable Truth	Advantages	Cross
Examination	Core Issues	Topic
Disadvantage	Decision	Calculus

Arguments operate within a framework of discussion. The last two chapters have explored two of those frameworks, *value and fact*. This chapter will focus upon the third framework, *policy*.

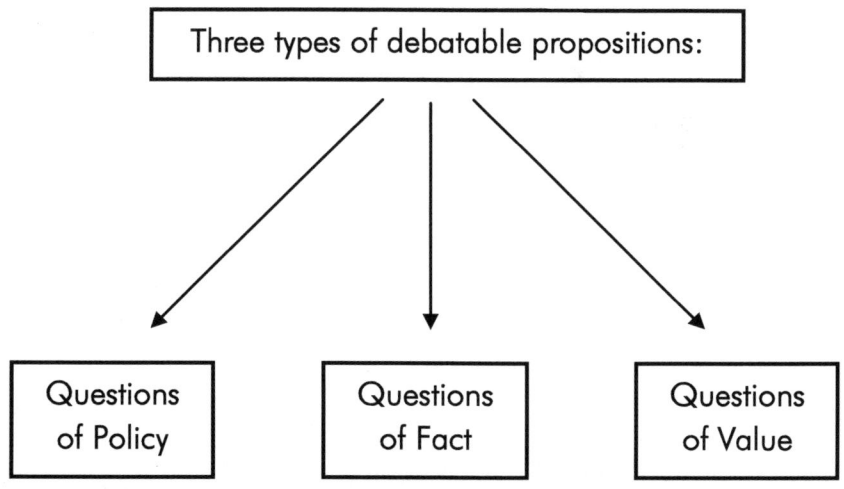

Debate in any format is really just a contest of argumentation. The format delineates the types of issues to be argued, but argumentation provides the infrastructure that propels the discussion.

Chapter Two looked at this infrastructure from a theoretical viewpoint. In this chapter, we will take the argument theory presented in that chapter and apply it to a framework of policy discussion.

What Is Included in a Policy Discussion?

Life seems to involve a continual series of questions. Should I go to college? What should I major in? Should I ask Sally to Homecoming? Do I want to go through the main line or just get a salad?

Each question requires a person to have some basic knowledge, to think or analyze that knowledge, and finally to draw some conclusions before responding to the question. Sometimes that process takes very little time, and we answer the question immediately.

Other times the answers require some time to think and maybe even seek some additional information or even advice.

Example:
Question: Where should I eat tonight?

Possibilities: McDonalds?   Wendy's?
                 Big Mac,   Double Cheeseburger,
                 French Fries   Frosty

In each of the questions above, the person is asked to **make a policy decision**. A policy decision amounts to choosing a course of action based upon information available. We make policy decisions all the time and don't even think about it. Most of these questions don't have an absolutely correct answer.

What is correct or what is true isn't a sure thing in all cases. In fact, some truth may be present on both sides of the question. The main line has some good food, and I like a lot of the items offered, but I also like salads. Salads have fewer calories, but I really wouldn't have to eat the potatoes on the main course. So, what should I choose?

The decision comes when the truth on all sides of the question are weighed and evaluated. In this example the discussion of the possibilities, **leads you to a particular course of action**.

The policy discussions that receive a lot of attention, especially around election time, come from politics. With elections happening every two years and with politicians starting their campaigns three or four years before an election, we often become numb from the constant appeals being made by our politicians daily.

Polls show that over half of our population have tired of the continual bickering and are tuning it out as much as is possible even to the point of staying home instead of voting.

Many see this constant haranguing as a continual loop without either a beginning or an end. Others get caught up in the issues being debated, passionately listen to the arguments being offered, and, like an avid football fan, offer their opinions to whoever will listen. Policy discussions sometimes seem void of real arguments and far from any search for truth.

Good argumentation involves **discussing and considering all the issues** involved with making a policy decision. Through argumentation, we can get a better understanding of the issues involved and make better decisions. It doesn't matter how simple the decision to be made is, or how complex. We all use some form of argumentation to aid in our decision making.

Sometimes we argue with ourselves, and sometimes we consult with another person. In the end, we consider all the truth that has been laid out and make our decision. Sometimes the road is crooked, but the arguments clear away the fog and lead us down the path to a decision.

Questions of policy inundate every facet of our lives and like everything else, the bad sometimes overshadows the good. Good policy discussions involving good argumentation provide clarity to things that are often unclear and are the basis of good policy decisions.

In this chapter, **our goal is to establish** a reliable process for making decisions while applying the ethical standard of searching for truth and the rhetorical structures outlined in Chapter Two.

The discussion turns into a debate and that is a good thing!

THE GOOD OF DEBATE

Debate is a format of discussion and the format we will use in this chapter. It is a popular format and is used in various structures for contests in both high school and college. Politicians use various forms of debate to show the differences between candidates on issues.

The heart of any debate is making **arguments**. While an argument, especially informal argument involve a process with lots of variables, arguments support the *core issues* associated with a policy decision making. Sounds complicated, doesn't it? Well, it isn't. In fact it is the way most logical people think without even thinking about it. The problem is that most people skip some of the steps.

Yes, arguments are used to support the *core issues* that exist within all policy decisions. An *issue* is a major point of concern within the question being discussed. There are several major points of concern (*core issues*) within each debatable question that call for a policy decision. That debatable question is called a **proposition**.

An example would be:

> How can we solve the problem of increasing violence in the United States?

Another example would be:

> Should I buy a car? Propositions usually cover very broad areas of concern.

The term *"core issue"* is often referred to as a *"stock issue."* For this book, the author chose to use the term **core** instead of **stock**. The reason is that the term *"stock issue"* has several connotations other than being the label for a **core or central** issue in a policy discussion. *"Stock issue"* is also used as the name of a system of evaluating a debate. To avoid confusion, the authors will use **core issue** as our label of choice for the major points of concern in a policy discussion.

Before effective debate can happen, it is often necessary to narrow the proposition down or at least make the question into a statement. In formal debate that statement is in the form of a **resolution** that could be presented to congress.

An example would be:

> *Resolved*: The United States federal government should set up an electronic registration for fire arms that can be easily shared with all law enforcement agencies within each State.

An example of a resolution in a more informal setting would be:

> *Resolved*: I should buy a new car.

A **resolution** establishes the boundaries for the clash of arguments within each issue and divides the arguments into two categories, yes or no. The figure below provides a visual look at how the issues and arguments of a policy debate break down.

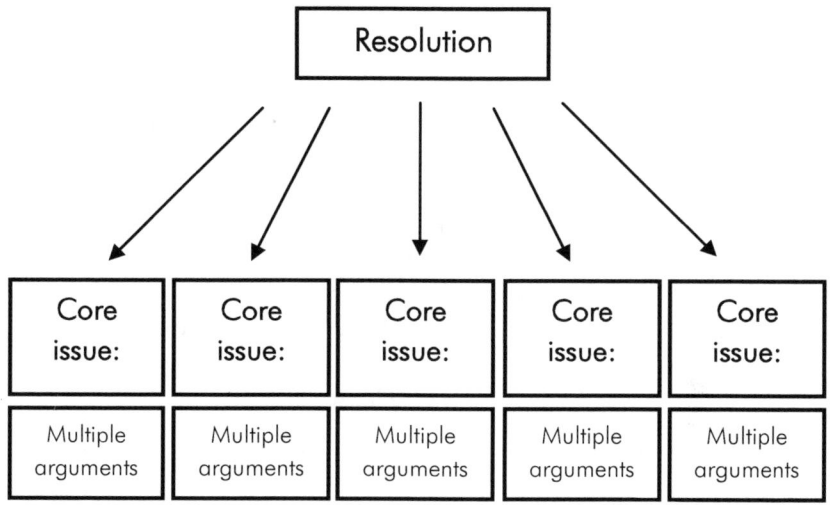

EXTERNAL PROCESS

Sounds complicated, doesn't it? Well, it isn't. In fact it is the way most logical people think without even thinking about it. The problem is that most people skip some of the steps. They don't see the external process as a whole. They see only many component parts that make up the internal process.

After completing this chapter, you will not only be aware of the steps in the external process of analyzing a policy question, but you will also be able to identify all the issues and arguments associated with a policy question. That way you will be able to sort through everything that was said and everything that was read and make sense of it.

So, when it comes time for you to make policy decisions, you won't be leaving out any steps in the process of analyzing the situation.

It doesn't matter if the policy question is to buy a new car or to change occupations; the basic analysis contains three areas of consideration. What is the **problem**? What is the **cause**? What is the **solution**?

These three questions must be answered in order to completely analyze a policy question. They form the external process for your analysis.

External Resolution Analysis
1. Problem
2. Cause
3. Solution

This external process forms the framework for all analysis and is the source for a solution. When problems arise that are significant enough to gain our attention. The solution to the problem will always be to get rid of the cause. This is true of all policy questions.

All external analysis begins with the resolution. A debate has two sides, the **affirmative** and the **negative,** or in the case of more informal situations, yes or no. The resolution statement forces the debater to take one of those two sides.

The argumentation, then, centers on a proposed resolution which calls for a new policy or a change in a policy within the present way of doing things **(status quo)**. The **affirmative** is for that resolution or would be on the side that would answer, **"Yes we need a new car."**

The **negative** is opposed to the resolution and would **say no to the resolution**. The resolution proposes that we change something in the present system, the **status quo**. Because it must support the resolution, the affirmative will present the change in the form of a policy. That policy is referred to as the affirmative plan in a formal debate.

Following our example from above, the Affirmative would propose a system for registering guns, and the Negative would either be against gun registration or propose a better way of solving for the violence. In the second portion of the example, the Affirmative would be for buying a new car, while the negative would be against the purchase.

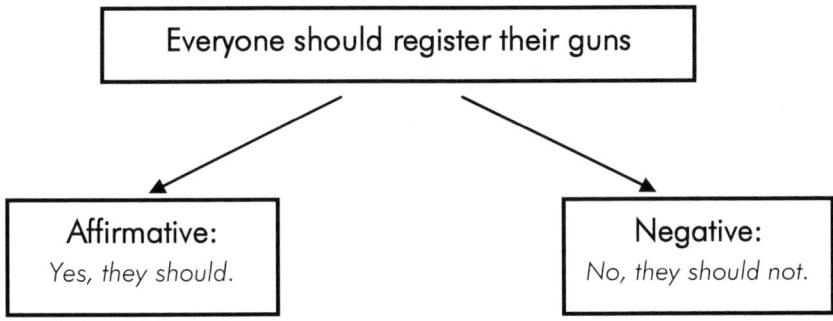

The affirmative will claim a **problem**. There is lots of gun violence. The affirmative will claim all the violence is related to not registering guns—the **cause** of the problem. The affirmative will then claim that the **solution** is to register guns. The negative will try to negate or oppose each of those claims. Remember the structure of an argument presented in Chapter Two.

Parts of an Argument

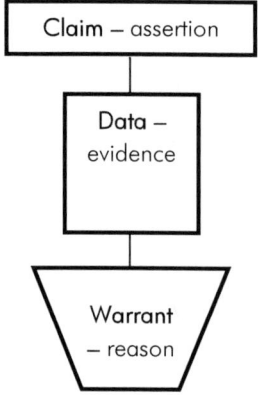

The claims of problem, cause, and solution are really headings for multiple arguments that support each of the three claims. These arguments and the issues they support will be discussed further under the heading of internal process. Each argument will delineate the truth within each issue.

It is important to understand that the resolutions being debated cannot be classified as absolutely true. If the resolution was absolutely true, there would be no debate. Truth will appear on both sides of the issues involved in a debate. It is the audience that will consider all the arguments and determine the truth for that particular time and place. As they consider the arguments, the audience will be immersed with likes and dislikes and all forms of biases.

At the end of the debate season, in the case of formal debate where several debates about one resolution take place, it is good to decide which side contains the most truth. After a season of debate, many of the debaters often have a new view of which side actually does contain the most truth. During a season of debate, research will provide new insight into just what is and is not the truth.

Also, presenting the arguments to different audiences will shape and color the issues within a debate and the arguments that are immersed within those issues. After running all the arguments through the many judge or audience filters a season of debate offers, a person can get a pretty good understanding of just what the probable truth is. This realization gives insight into Perelman's theory of audience that was discussed in Chapter Two.

Informally, debate is considering all the possible arguments associated with a desired course of action. An example would be choosing a restaurant. A person would consider the type of food served, the quality of the food, the price of the food, and the delivery system, just to name a few.

All of these considerations could be made into arguments for or against eating at an establishment. Formal debate allows us to examine the elements within the process of making a policy decision in a more structured setting. This process can be applied to informal situations, but can be best seen in the formal setting.

Therefore, our discussion will center on formal policy debate. We have looked at the external process involved—problem, cause, and solution. Now, we will look at the internal process—those *core issues* we talked of earlier.

THE INTERNAL PROCESS

In a policy debate, each side, negative and affirmative, will divide all of their arguments into the *core issues* involved. Yes, in policy debate, only a certain number of issues are possible and all arguments will apply to those *core issues*. The affirmative arguments will support all those issues in relation to adopting the resolution, and the negative arguments will support all those issues in relation to opposing the adoption of the resolution.

The affirmative is for a change in the status quo. In formal debate, the change that the affirmative wants is the **resolution**. The affirmative then asks that we adopt a **plan** (policy) that will implement that change. If this sounds like a huge task, it becomes easier when the *core issues* are identified. In policy decisions, only a set number of issues need to be considered. That is true in every policy decision, big or small.

PROBLEM

To start the process, the affirmative must convince the audience (judge) that the **change they want is needed or justified.** In other words, the affirmative must show that there is some "reason for a change." Solving a *problem* that makes the proposed policy at least somewhat better than the current policy (*status quo*) can provide that *justification*.

The affirmative does this by showing that there is something wrong (*Harm*) with status quo that needs repair, and by showing that adopting the affirmative plan will have some great consequences or benefits (eliminating the harms-**Solvency**) that debaters call *advantages*. *Harm* is one of the *core issues*.

Another element of *justification* is the *significance* of the problem. Problems that that exist below the surface of consciousness don't warrant attention. A tire's tread will gradually wear until it becomes dangerous. That wear is not significant until it becomes dangerous. Determining the significance of a problem will help establish the justification of fixing the problem. Significance is another core issue.

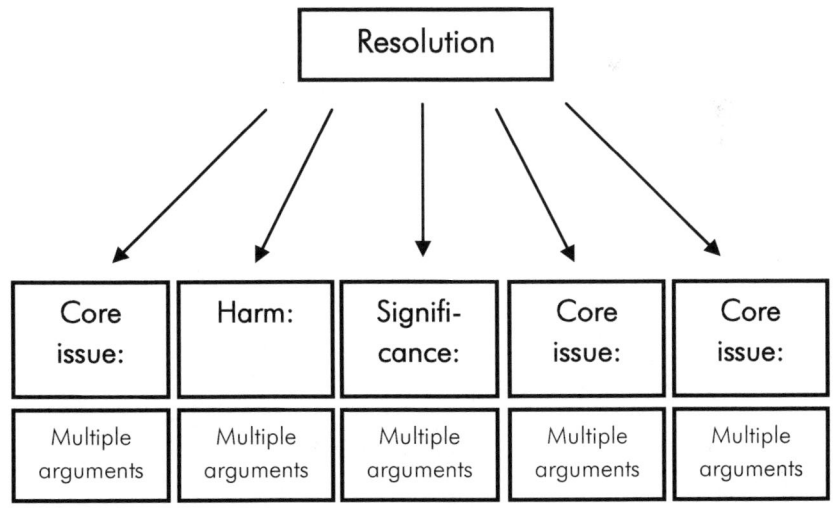

The affirmative can look at several areas to find (**justification or need for a change) in the proposal being offered**. They can look for **problems, what is wrong (harms),** within the **social** areas of our life.

Examples might be that crime is causing people to live in fear, or that large numbers of people are smoking which leads to a higher death rate. These, then, become arguments to support the core issue of harm. Looking at the problems **(harms)** within the **economic** areas of life produces a possibility of more arguments to support the core issue of harm.

An example might be that lots of people are poor and can't feed their families, or that large oil companies are inflating oil prices and causing people with low incomes to not have money for health insurance. Finally, the affirmative could look at the problems **(harms)** within the **political** areas of the world where still more arguments are possible.

Another example might be how other countries of the world see the USA as always trying to enforce their will on them, or how our system of government in the United States forces the individual states to accept whatever "Big Brother" wants.

By pointing out these problems **(harms)** and showing the positive consequences of solving for the harms **(advantages)**, the affirmative provides the necessary information needed to convince the judge that there is justification for the change proposed, that the change (plan) is really needed.

To further sub divide the analysis of the problem, we will label these two considerations *harm* and *significance*. If we are considering buying a new car, the argument that the car we now drive breaks down all the time supports the **harm**, and the costs of repairs and being late to work are arguments that constitute the level of **significance** this problem has. We call this **quantitative significance**.

However, significance doesn't always depend upon numbers. Sometimes the significance depends upon what is right or wrong, or it depends on what has value in a person's life. That can be tougher to see. For instance, an argument can be made that the act of our neighbors buying a new car can also be harmful.

Everyone wants to "fit in" with the people we think are important in our lives. If everyone in the neighborhood is driving a new car and we are driving a piece of junk, it can be embarrassing. How much we are embarrassed also constitutes arguments supporting the **significance** of the problem. We call this **qualitative significance**. What is significant to you may not be significant to me.

In both cases, **quantitative significance and qualitative significance**, the question is if the harm is significant enough to spend the resources required to buy the car.

Internal Resolution Analysis
1. Problem
    a. Harm

      b. Significance
          i. Quantitative Significance
          ii. Qualitative Significance
2. Cause
3. Solution

Cause

Another element of *justification* is cause. If there is no cause to a problem, a solution cannot be justified. When considering **the cause** of the problem, it is possible to subdivide the analysis into several areas of possible arguments.

For instance, if the **cause** of the problem is a faulty spark plug, it would be cheaper to buy a new spark plug than to buy a new car. On the other hand, if the cause of the problem is that the engine blew up; arguments might be made that it would be cheaper in the long run to buy the new car. These causes are **structural** in nature and can be fixed by simply changing the structure, buying a spark plug, a new engine, or a new car.

Another argument could be that if the old car was already on a maintenance program with the car dealership, and the dealership said that upon completion of that program the car would be good for another 50,000 miles, that maintenance program might take away the problem altogether.

One of the considerations when looking at the causes of the problem for possible arguments is to look at the current solutions being applied. If current solutions being offered (current structures) are working, why do we need to adopt a new one, buy a new car? Current structures designed to help alleviate the problem are considered *structural inherency*.

Sometimes the problem is because of **attitudes**. An example of an argument in this area is if the person wanting a new car did not take care of the previous one, would buying a new car change anything.

A new car could have the same problems if the owner did not take care of it. If the oil wasn't checked regularly or if no maintenance was ever done, buying a new car might just be a waste of money. The solution would include more than just buying a car. It would include changing some **attitudes**.

In the case of the person who does not own a car in the first place, but who needs transportation, the cause of the problem is because of a **void or gap** in options available to solve the problem. The solution to the problem would then have to include new structure. Arguments would revolve around the new owner doing new things. The person would have to buy the car, get insurance, maybe get a driver's license, and buy a tag. Those are things that would be new to that person.

In looking at the *cause* of the problem, many people ask the question, "What keeps us from solving the problem?" Those causes are often called **barriers** to solving the problem. The basic *"barriers"* are **structure**, **attitudes**, and **gaps** (in the existing structure).

The issue associated with the *cause* of the problem is called **inherency**. Inherency is a term that refers to the permanence of the problem.

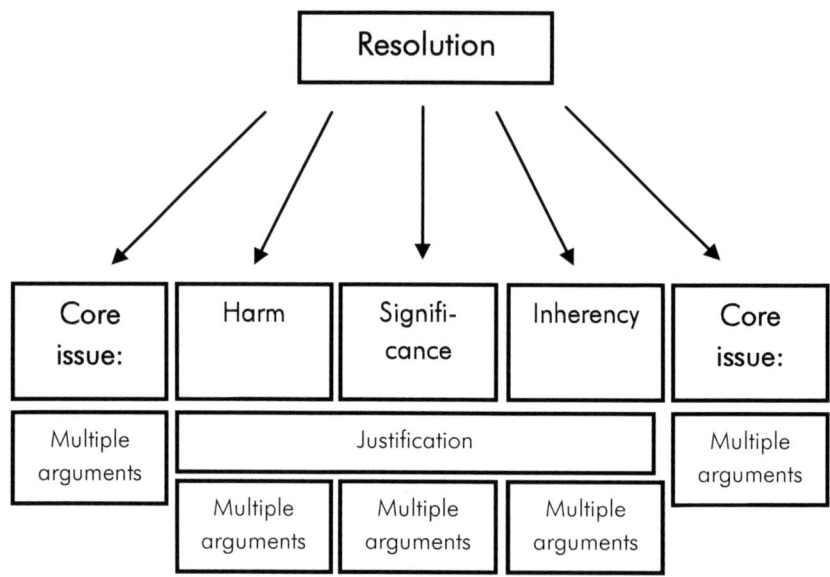

Another look at *inherency* would be to look at what is already being done to solve a problem. This could provide god negative argumentation. In some cases the present system is already working on the problem. In other words there are **current solutions** being tried.

It would not be good to try to solve a problem until the **current solution** has had a chance to work or has been in existence long enough to verify its solvency. An affirmative plan would then not be needed if the status quo already has a policy that is working.

Another area for finding arguments when analyzing the problem from an inherency perspective is ***alternate causality***. Sometimes the discussion of the possibility of buying a new car focuses upon causes that really aren't directly causing the problem. For instance, if you want a new car so you won't be late to work, you need to consider all the causes of why you are late. Most people would point to the time the car wouldn't start.

However, maybe a new alarm clock or a few new parts for your car would solve the problem without having to buy a new one. To work, solutions must address the causes of problems. Debaters must make sure that all the causes are addressed, or the solution won't work as efficiently as it could.

Internal Resolution Analysis
1. Problem
    a. Harm
    b. Significance
        i. Quantitative Significance
        ii. Qualitative Significance
2. Cause (**Inherency**)
    a. Barriers
        i. Structural
        ii. Attitudinal
        iii. Void or Gap
    b. Current Solutions
    c. Alternate Causality
3. Solution

Solution
The **solution** to the problem must also be analyzed and subdivided. The first consideration concerning the solution is if

the *solution will actually solve* the problem. This is often called **Plan Meets Need**. The solution (**plan**) must actually **solve** (**meet**) the problem (**need** for a change).

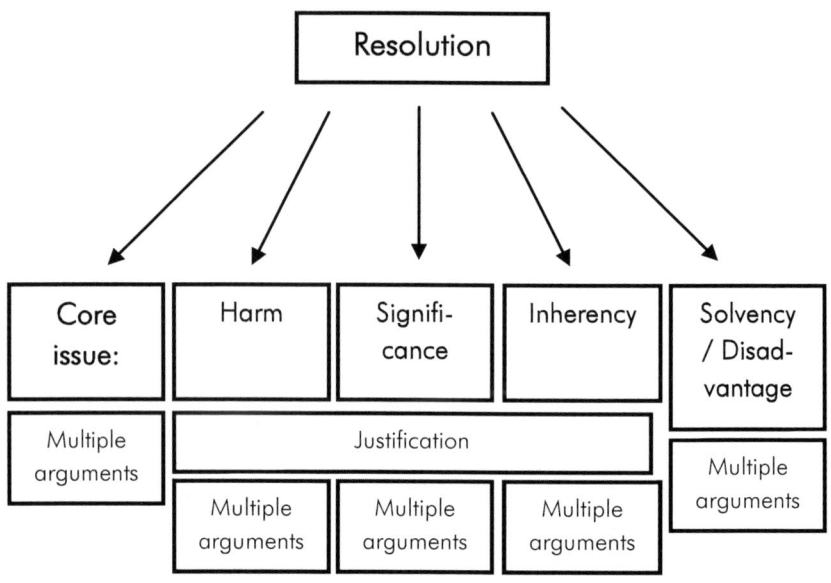

In order for the **plan to meet the need,** it must be determined if *the plan addresses all of the causes*. If one of the reasons (causes) for the car not running well is that it misses out and is difficult to start, then the plan needs to address the cause of that. If it can be fixed cheaply, then maybe a new car is not needed. Arguments can be made both for and against to support (PMN) plan meets need.

Also, the *plan has to work* for the **plan to meet the need**. Many arguments come out of this analysis. If you don't have the money to buy a new car, the plan won't solve. If you buy a used (new to you) car and it has mechanical problems, the plan won't solve. Lots of things could keep a solution from working.

A debater should consider all of them, but only those workability issues that threaten the ability of the plan to solve are important enough to mention in a debate.

Another area for arguments in analyzing **plan meets need** (PMN) is something called *circumvention*. If a person inherits a new car, it would not be necessary to buy a new car. If a car pool is available or if public transportation exists, then a new car would not be needed to get to work. The problem has been circumvented by another solution outside the resolution.

Next, someone besides a high school student has to recommend this plan. The audience will need more than just a debater's word that the *plan is legitimate.* Arguments from this analysis come from two different sources. One is by **advocacy** and the other is through **empirical support**. **Advocacy** means that someone who has expertise within the area being discussed supports the proposed solution.

This **advocate** must have expertise and should be minimally biased. **Empirical support** comes from the plan being used somewhere else or for something else. **Empirical support** could also come from scientific study dealing with a similar or like situation. **Every solution, *plan*, must be legitimized by either advocacy or through empirical support.**

Finally, let us assume that the plan passes and that it does work. If all that happens, can some bad things happen as well?

If a new car is purchased but the payments are so large that a person can't pay the rent, that is a bad thing. Bad side effects that result from the passage of the plan are called **disadvantages**.

Each disadvantage is an argument against passing the plan. If the bad impacts of the **disadvantages** outweigh the good impacts of the **advantages** that comes from the plan, then the plan should not be adopted.

The **probability** of the disadvantage even happening, the **time frame** it takes for the impact to happen, and the **magnitude** of the impact are the main considerations in that decision. **Time frame** and **probability** determine the **risk** of the impact happening.

If the **solvency** of the plan could cause disadvantages, it would be good to know before the plan is adopted. Therefore, a major area of analysis in a debate of policy is what problems will the solvency of the plan produce.

Disadvantages can come from two different situations. Sometimes a policy just makes things worse. These are called **linear disadvantages** because they show an increase in *severity* of an existing harm. Other times a policy can bring on new problems. These are called **unique disadvantages** because they only happen when a specific policy is in effect.

Linear disadvantages are often easily found. An example would be buying a new car. I already am in debt with a car loan and the payments are difficult to make. Going in debt for a new car with higher payments makes it more difficult. It might not put me into bankruptcy, but it will mean that I won't be able to go out to eat as often or maybe not have a night out at the movies. I will not feel new pain, but I will feel more of the old pain.

Linear DA

These disadvantages are more difficult to quantify or show the **magnitude**. Often the harm presented in the disadvantage can only be shown through the loss of quality of life: loss of going to a movie or loss of freedom.

Example:

> Every time a federal law is passed in opposition to federalism, individual freedom is lost. The impacts of linear disadvantages are not terminal, but the pain is real never the less. However, the magnitude from the impacts of linear disadvantages is usually less than with *unique disadvantages*.

The ability to show the effect the policy has upon the impact of a linear disadvantage determines the *propensity* or **probability** of that argument.

To show the effect of the policy upon the impact quantitatively, it is necessary to show the relationship of the increase in pain to the policy.

Example:

> For every $100 spent on social programs, we lose 200 jobs. To show the qualitative effects of the policy, it is necessary to identify the losses to quality of life.

Example:

> I will no longer have the choice of which doctor I see. The government will choose my doctor for me by the limits they place on my health care plan.

Linear Disadvantage:
  A. Link (How the policy causes the disadvantage)
  B. Effect of Policy upon Disadvantage
  C. Impact (The harm caused by the new policy)

If the new policy is the straw that "breaks the camel's back" or is the cause of a huge rush of harmful things, then, the policy puts us over the **"brink."** This type of linear disadvantage is called a **linear brink disadvantage,** it happens or it doesn't happen.

In the example of buying a new car, the increase in payments make it so I can't pay my bills and the result is bankruptcy. This type of **linear disadvantage** provides more **magnitude** to the impact.

Time frame is not a consideration since the impact is immediate.

Linear Brink Disadvantage:
- A. Link
- B. Brink
    - a. Status quo is near the brink.
    - b. The new policy pushes us over the edge.
- C. Impact

The **unique disadvantage** is sometimes called a *threshold* disadvantage because the new policy puts us on a path toward bad things. Sometimes the impact will come immediately, but more often the new policy will initiate the action that leads toward the impact. The length of that path is called a *time frame*.

A shorter time frame means that the harms of the disadvantage will come sooner. The less threshold the more unique the disadvantage. However, the longer the path, the more possible it is that something would come along and stop the impact.

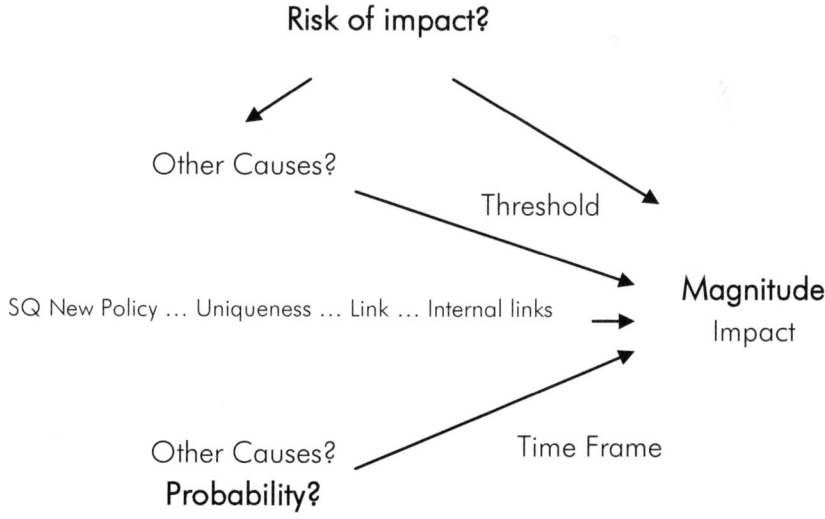

That *time frame* is therefore related to the **uniqueness** of the disadvantage. Why is it important for a disadvantage to be unique? If a disadvantage could be caused by something else, then it becomes more difficult to attribute the harm solely to the new policy.

That disadvantage is then less *intrinsic*; the impact does not come entirely from the new policy or some other policy could cause the impact before the new policy. That is why **linear disadvantages** have less **magnitude** than **unique disadvantages**.

Unique Disadvantage
A. Uniqueness (Status quo is doing well without the new policy)
B. Link (What part or parts of the new policy cause this disadvantage.) (Trigger)
C. Internal link (Why will the new policy cause the impact?) (Threshold)
D. Impact (The harm caused by the new policy)

If all this discussion of things like *uniqueness* and *intrinsicness* is confusing, it important to remember the bigger picture. The focus is on a policy decision; should we or should we not adopt this new policy.

To answer that question, the core issues must be considered. In this case the core issue is solvency. One argument that can be made to discredit **solvency** is the **disadvantage**, negative side effects of the new policy

Therefore, what is being evaluated is if the advantages of the plan outweigh the disadvantages it causes. Because this whole process is so full of variables and the outcome is not absolute, it is necessary to weigh risks, the **risk** of the advantages of the new policy against the **risk** of the disadvantages.

It is also necessary to weigh the *magnitude* of each. Much of that **risk** evaluation, along with *magnitude*, centers upon the *probability,* and *time frame* of the impacts of the disadvantage. Impacts basically divide into two categories, *terminal* and *non-terminal*.

Terminal impacts lead to death, extinction or anything that cannot be recovered from. It is a trend in competitive debate to only use **terminal impacts** because the *magnitude* of the impact can outweigh advantages. There are two problems with **terminal impacts**. One is that unless the link story is really convincing, it is a difficult sale. The *probability* that the impact will actually happen is very low, and the *time frame* is forever. That lowers the *risk* of the impact ever happening.

Will buying a new car actually cause nuclear war? How long will it take? The other problem is that both sides can play the same game. If those arguing for the new policy use **terminal impacts** for the advantages, how can you weigh total destruction over total destruction? If we are not going to live either way, who cares? What is the *risk* of the impact happening?

Non-terminal impacts are negative consequences that may not have as large of magnitude and are can often be survived. A **non-terminal impact** could be job loss, hunger, lower profits or any other negative side effect which may potentially overcome.

It is good to make those impacts appear the most painful. For instance, having to take on another job would mean less time with the family. That could lead to marriage problems or behavior problems with the kids. All those impacts are bad but **non terminal**.

Solvency arguments are basic to the question of all policy decisions. If buying that car won't relieve the problems, or if solving the problems causes more problems, the question becomes, "Is it worth it?" Many times a debate will come down to a weighing of advantages of the plan versus the disadvantages caused by the plan. The advantages come from plan solvency that produces good results and disadvantages come from plan solvency that produces bad results.

Internal Resolution Analysis
1. Problem
    a. **Harm**
    b. Significance
        i. Quantitative Significance
        ii. Qualitative Significance
2. Cause (**Inherency**)
    a. Barriers
        i. Structural
        ii. Attitudinal

iii. Void or Gap
   1. Current Solutions
   2. Alternate Causality
3. Solution
   a. Plan Meets Need (**Solvency**)
      i. Plan addresses all of the causes
      ii. Plan workability
      iii. Circumvention
      iv. Plan legitimacy
         1. Advocacy
         2. Empirical support
   b. Disadvantages
      i. Linear
      ii. Unique

TOPICALITY

One *core issue* remains. I have waited to present it last because it does not deal with the substance of the resolution. This core issue is *topicality*. It is called a *procedural issue*, while the other four are called *substantive issues*.

Just because I mention it last does not mean that it is of lesser importance. In fact, it is called **A Priori** which means that it should be the first issue that is argued in every speech if it exists. The other *core issues* exist in every policy, but *topicality* exists only when there is a violation or misuse. It is a procedural issue because *topicality* refers to the ground rules of the debate.

Every word in the resolution has a definition or more than one definition. In other words, **each word has a meaning.** How a team defines those words (the meaning of the word) establishes the boundaries of the resolution. Some may choose to use a little known definition to limit or expand the size of the topics included within the resolution.

For example, in the resolution that I should buy a new car, someone could define car to include truck. If car was defined that way, I could propose that I buy a big rig to transport cattle. That would allow me areas to explore that I couldn't if car was defined only as a car.

Those areas are referred to as *ground*. Arguments will come from the loss or gain of ground.

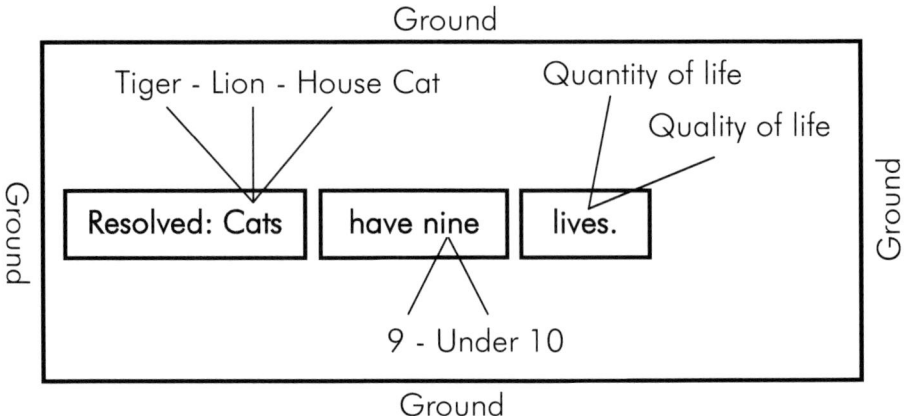

In the *Figure* above, choosing one definition over another would skew the ground one way or another. Only research would tell you if there is more evidence in favor of Tigers having 9 lives or not. The same is true for quality of life as quality of life doesn't talk about death but how well life is lived.

In a debate **it is good if the ground** (areas for exploration) **is evenly divided** between affirmative and negative. In the example of buying a new car given earlier, the affirmative (buying a big rig) has expanded the ground in favor of the affirmative. The negative will have to be able to defend something that a reasonable person might not think of when thinking about cars. The negative might not be prepared to argue about "big rigs." This would give the affirmative an advantage.

Both negative and affirmative should look closely at all possible definitions and the possible interpretations of each. This is a *dialectic* approach. In that way both teams will be prepared to argue the issue of topicality.

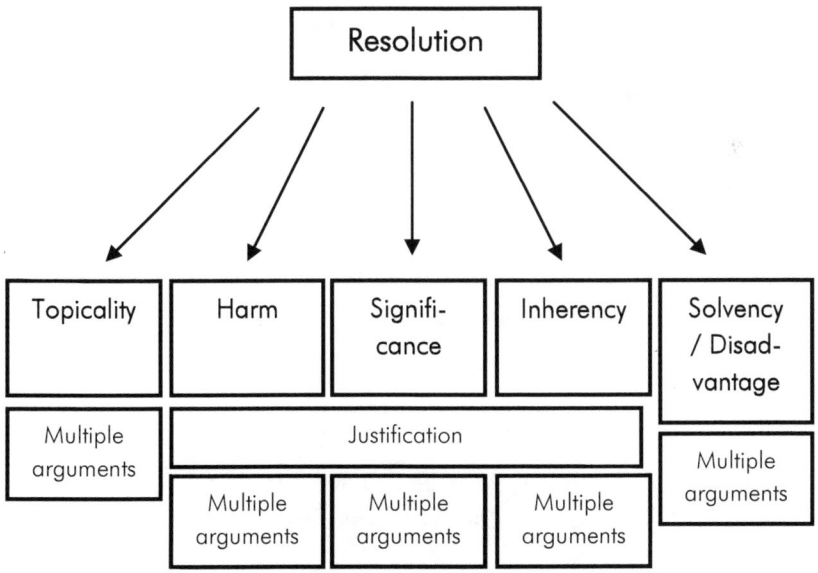

Ground and advantage is what the topicality issue is all about. Debaters often argue the definitions used as to their *reasonability*. If the affirmative uses a definition that is unreasonable, the negative is put in a disadvantageous situation. The negative may not be able to argue many of the points because they won't be prepared. The negative would say that the definition used was not predictable, and so it had not been researched by the negative.

The debate itself would then become a farce and any educational value from that debate would be lost. Of course, if the terms are defined in a reasonable way, the negative would have nothing to complain about. If they were not prepared, it would be their fault.

Debaters will argue one of two **measuring calculi** called **standards or reasons to prefer.** One is *reasonableness,* which we discussed above. The other *standard* is *best definition*. The **best definition standard** argues that to get the best understanding of the resolution, it is important to use the best definition of a term.

To establish that the affirmative is not either a **reasonable** interpretation or the **best interpretation**, the negative will offer a **counter definition** which will better meet the appropriate standard. They will then compare the definition offered by the affirmative with the definition they offered.

This comparison is the basis of the topicality argument. It is often not an easy decision as to if the affirmative is **reasonable** or the **best**. Another **measuring calculus** is needed. A set of criteria called micro standards are used to help determine.

Micro Standards are reasons why one definition is more **reasonable** or is the **best definition** in the round. For instance, in some cases a definition from a law dictionary might be better than one from Webster. In another instance, it might be better to use a definition from an expert. In another it might be better to use a definition that is universally understood by everyone.

Topicality, then, is debated around the definitions of the words used in the resolution. Both teams will try to establish that their interpretation of the resolution (through their use of words within the resolution) is **reasonable or best**. The outcome should produce a fair debate over the **substantive issues** within the resolution.

The last set of arguments pertain to the **impact of this core issue** upon the whole decision making process. At times topicality is so important that all the substantive issues do not matter. If a person's interpretation of the resolution is so unreasonable that it is not relevant to the subject in hand, that interpretation should be rejected. In competition debate rounds, this would be a reason for a judge to vote against the affirmative in the round. In competition debate, this argument is called a **voter**. That means that the issue as presented is so important, the adjudicator should vote against the affirmative.

Other times the issue of topicality does not rise to that level. The arguments made at each structure level will determine if the impact rises to that level. Usually, in a competitive debate, those arguments on impact revolve around fairness and ground which we discussed earlier. Was the negative team given a fair chance? Because the negative had only limited research, did the arguments go deep enough into the issues to provide an educational result for the students involved?

Another consideration could be jurisdiction. The adjudicator or judge of the round has certain guidelines to follow, depending upon which format of debate was being utilized. In some cases, those guidelines call for the judge to vote against the affirmative if the negative wins the issue.

Topicality

A. Violation – what specific term or phrase is in question and how it is being used. (It is usually defined by the Affirmative contextually and will have to be interpreted.)

B. Counter Definition – what is a better definition and why. (A counter definition is offered and analysis as to why it is a better definition.)

C. Standard or Reasons to Prefer– a way to measure one term above another in relation to the macro standard. (These criteria or reasons to prefer, are needed to determine which definition is best. These criteria might center on the definition itself or the grammatical context, or field context, or any number of criteria that would help determine which definition is reasonable or best.)

D. Voter/impact — why this issue is important in this round (Since topicality is a procedural issue, it must be decided first. Thus, topicality is always argued at the beginning of a speech. It can be important enough to warrant the judges' vote regardless of the other issues. To be that important, it would have to be the cause of an **unfair distribution of ground** making it difficult for one side or the other or **violate the jurisdictional boundaries** established for the debate.)

Internal Resolution Analysis

1. Topicality
    a. Violation
    b. Counter Definition
    c. Standards or Reasons to Prefer
    d. Voter/Impact
2. Problem
    a. **Harm**
    b. Significance
        i. Quantitative Significance
        ii. Qualitative Significance
3. Cause (**Inherency**)
    a. Barriers
        i. Structural
        ii. Attitudinal
        iii. Void or Gap
    b. Current Solutions
    c. Alternate Causality

4. Solution
    a. Plan Meets Need (**Solvency**)
        i. Plan addresses all of the causes
        ii. Plan workability
        iii. Circumvention
        iv. Plan legitimacy
            1. Advocacy
            2. Empirical support
    b. Disadvantages
        i. Linear
        ii. Unique

Another procedural argument that arises with the discussion of passing plan is that of fiat. Fiat does not rise to the level of a core issue, but it is a procedural argument, and as such, it should be dealt with ahead of the substantive arguments. It has nothing to do with the substance of the debate. It is entirely about process. The argument is **will the plan will pass**.

When the debate is over, the plan won't actually be in effect. In days past, negative would focus argument on the possibility of actually passing plan. Those arguments lead us away from important issues that formed the basis of the debate. In order to keep the argumentation focused upon the substantive issues, it became necessary to reach a friendly agreement with those debating to eliminate debate on whether congress would actually pass the affirmative proposal.

This agreement is **fiat**. Fiat means that the affirmative does not have to prove that the plan will pass congress.

Affirmatives often evolve this friendly agreement into **"Fiat Power."** Claiming automatic approval of everything from fiat is not the intention of that friendly agreement. Affirmatives have been known to claim fiat for funds that are not available, and technology that has not been invented. Fiat applies only to the passing of plan and not the guarantying of solvency. Arguing fiat in a debate often confuses judges and turns the debate into a haggle.

However, sometimes its improper use by the affirmative can skew a round to the point that solvency is automatically awarded to the affirmative. To argue this, the negative should not argue fiat, but instead, offer a disadvantage that shows the harms of doing exactly what the affirmative wants to be done. If the affirmative tries to fiat money, the negative should show how harmful it is to take the money from something else.

If the negative attempts to require the affirmative to prove that congress will pass the plan, the affirmative should frame their arguments around the word "should" in the resolution. Policy resolutions always have that word in them as a result of that friendly agreement. The word should means that something ought to be done. It does not mean something has to be done.

Application—Congressional Debate

Using this external and internal analysis gives a complete look at a situation and exposes all the truth. At that point, a person can intelligently consider courses of action (solutions) that are appropriate. Most people use some or all of this process to make decisions, but leaving out part of the process relegates outcomes to a matter of luck instead of reasoned thinking.

This process can be accomplished by a single person or as a group process. Most businesses have found that using small groups of people to solve problems is advantageous. Committees are commonplace throughout the business world because they work.

When people work together and communicate well, exciting things often happen. By bouncing ideas off each other, new insights come into view and the seemingly impossible becomes possible. This invisible but documentable force that causes problems to be solved in small groups has come to be called synergy.

Many different approaches have been offered to aid those small groups in solving problems. They are usually offered as a step by step process. The common thread in all of those approaches is the external structure presented in this chapter—quantifies the **problem,** identify the **causes,** and find all possible **solutions**.

Example
It has been a scary thing that so many acts of violence have occurred in the past few years. People have reacted with different ideas for a solution. Most of these solutions are products of emotion and reactions instead of well thought out ideas. Applying the external and internal analysis that was

discussed would give a more balanced look at all of the issues involved.

To do this, we will follow the format used in the Congress of The United States. The area of concern is violence. It is necessary to establish a proposition or question of concern. To do this, we need to put the problem in the form of a question. This will give an initial look at possible areas of concern. From this we can narrow or expand our topic for discussion to be most relevant.

Propositions should be in the form of a question and general enough to cover all the concerns. **How can we stop violence in the United States?** This proposition allows us to separate the problem into various concerns. For instance, we could concentrate on all violence, or we could limit it to school violence, or domestic violence, or violence committed with a gun. Other areas could be isolated as well.

Each area or groups of areas could be the subject of the next step, which is to format our ideas for discussion as a *resolution* suitable to be debated by Congress. If we choose to discuss school violence and guns, those two areas should be included in our resolution.

To do this we must present a solution within the statement as that helps us to divide the arguments into yes or no. One solution offered by some was to arm the teachers.

Was this reactionary or well thought out? The best way to find out is to debate the resolution. **Resolved**: All public schools should train and arm their teachers. Notice the word should. It means we ought to, but it doesn't mean we will. This allows us to run everything through our external and internal analysis. We will expose all the arguments and discover the truth on both sides of the resolution. Once that has been accomplished, congress will often offer a **Bill** which has the force of law. A Bill says we <u>will</u> do something.

Competitive congressional debate exists in both high school and college settings. While the numbers of opportunities for congressional debate are far less than with competitive policy debate, high school and collegiate opportunities for this type of competition are available.

This format will provide a good format to visualize the internal resolution analysis previously discussed. Competitive congressional debate starts the debate with an authorship speech in favor of the resolution. Speeches opposing the resolution and speeches affirming the resolution then follow in order. Speeches are three minutes in length followed with a time of questioning from the chamber. The debate continues until it is determined by the chamber that the issues are clear enough that the members can vote intelligently.

Each speech takes a core issue and express from one to three arguments in support of the speakers position on the issue. The order in which each core issue is dealt with is completely random. Each speaker vie for recognition from a presiding officer, and when called upon makes the arguments that concern the speaker. It is better when the speeches flow together, but it isn't mandatory.

Analysis of the resolution provides the framework for research that will aid the writing of speeches. It will also provide us with a good format to apply the internal resolution analysis to the Resolution: **Resolved**: All public schools should train and arm their teachers.

Internal Resolution Analysis

Core Issue:

Harm:
1. what are the social harms?
   - Families are devastated
   - Communities are divided
2. What are the Political harms?
   - Current laws are not working
   - New laws make schools gun free
3. What are the economic harms?
   - Cost of security
   - Opportunity costs

Significance:

Quantitative—
- How many incidents?
- How many killed?
- How much does it cost?

Qualitative—
- Not feeling safe
- Blame and guilt
- Break down of the family

Inherency:
Structural Barriers—
- Current laws—gun free zones; lack of enforcement
- New laws

Attitudinal Barriers—
- Attitude toward guns
- Attitude toward 2nd Amendment

Gap—
- Lack of data base of the mentally ill for background checks

Solvency:
Alternate Causality—
- Is something else causing the harm?
- Does it deal with the mentally ill?

Workability—
- What will it take to make this work?
- Who trains the teacher?
- What is included in the training?

Circumvention—
- How can I get around the law?
- What about private schools or charter schools?

Legitimacy—
- Who advocate this?
- Has it been tried before?

Disadvantages—
- Innocent people killed
- Attitude for learning destroyed

- Opportunity costs—problems of the mentally ill ignored

This *dialectic* exercise in the analysis of the resolution provides the frame work for the research that is necessary to *invent* the arguments available to support the core issues. Applying the research to the **starting points** exposed in the *dialectic* exercise above will provide ample arguments for each core issue.

Another competitive debate format is policy debate. Many different formats for competitive policy exist. National Debate Tournament (NDT), Cross Examination Debate Association (CEDA), National Forensics Association (NFA) Lincoln Douglas Debate and National Parliamentary Debate Tournament (NPDA) are the major formats in college that typically engage in policy debate. High school policy debate follows a similar format. The National Forensics League (NFL), Catholic Forensics League (CFL), and the National Federation of High School Activities Associations provide the rule base. Parliamentary Debate, Public Debate, and Public Forum also provide formats for competitive policy debate at the high school level.

APPLICATION—COMPETITIVE POLICY DEBATE

Competitive Policy Debate, as is true with all forms of competitive debate, is a contest of argumentation. A debate has two sides, the **affirmative** and the **negative**. Some formats have two people on a side and others have only one. In most formats, a debate will have to debate both sides.

The argumentation centers on a proposed resolution which calls for a new policy or a change in a policy within the status quo. The **affirmative** is for that resolution. The **negative** is opposed to the resolution. The resolution proposes that we change something in the present system, the **status quo**. Because it must support the resolution, the affirmative will present the change in the form of a policy. That policy is referred to as the affirmative plan in a competitive debate.

As we outlined earlier, informally debate involves considering all the possible arguments associated with a desired course of action. An example would be choosing a restaurant. A person would consider the type of food served, the quality of the food, the price of the food, and the delivery system, just to name a few. All of these considerations could be made into arguments for or against eating at an establishment.

Formal competitive debate allows us to be the advocate for one side, affirmative or negative. This allows the debaters to deeply examine the core issues and their arguments for each side. An adjudicator or judge then listens to arguments presented by each side and makes a decision.

Unlike the informal settings most people find themselves in the decision making process, competitive debate places the process of making a policy decisions in a more structured setting.

Congressional debate gave us a more specific look at the debate process Now, competitive policy debate will take a more intensive look at this process. Our discussion begins by examining the two sides.

THE AFFIRMATIVE

The affirmative is for a change in the status quo. In competitive policy debate, the change that the affirmative wants is the **resolution**. The affirmative then asks that we adopt a **plan** (policy) that will implement that change.

Three Basic Obligations

The **first** obligation of the affirmative is **justification**. The affirmative must convince the judge that the **change they want is needed or justified**. In other words, the affirmative must show that there is some "reason for a change" that makes the proposed policy worth adopting. Remember our discussion of problem, cause, solution? The core issues of harm, significance, and inherency provide the arguments that prove or disprove *justification*.

The affirmative does this by making arguments that something is wrong (**Harm**) with the status quo that needs repair, and by showing that adopting the affirmative plan will have some great consequences or benefits (eliminating the harms: **Solvency**) that debaters call *advantages* (**Significance**). Finally, the affirmative will need to show the causes of the problem by identifying the *inherent barrier* (Structural, attitudinal, or gap).

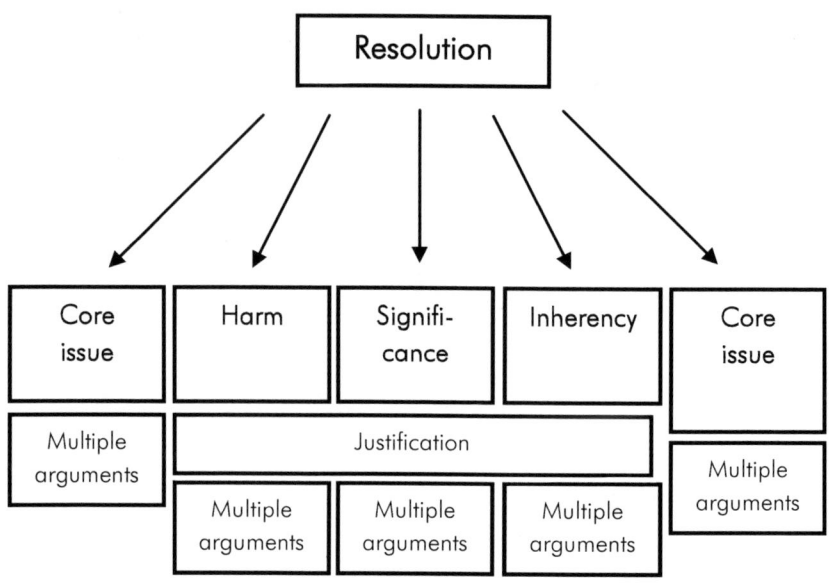

By pointing out these problems (**harms**), by showing the advantages or positive consequences of solving for the harms (**Significance**), and by sowing that the causes (**Inherency**) have been identified; the affirmative provides the necessary information needed to convince the judge that there is **justification** for the change proposed, that the change (plan) is really needed.

The *second obligation* of the affirmative is **burden of proof**. When the judge walks into the room, everything is operating by the rules in place that day (**Status Quo**). The **Affirmative** starts the debate by presenting the *Affirmative Case*. The **Affirmative** is going to ask everyone to *change* the rules or policy and adopt something different. The *change* the affirmative is proposing is the resolution. If the resolution is Resolved: Bill should buy a new car, the **affirmative** will say that he should and the **negative** will say he shouldn't.

In a criminal case, the prosecution lawyer has to present enough of a case in a grand jury or pre-trial hearing that the judge and jury would believe that the case needs to go to trial. The **Affirmative** has the same responsibility. That responsibility is called *prima facie*.

Prima Facie means that at first glance and without anyone giving opposing views, a reasonable person suspects that there is guilt. In the case of debate, the reasonable person is the judge and guilt is justification. The first affirmative speech must have presented enough arguments that a reasonable person will say at the end of the first speech that the affirmative is justified. That is **affirmative's** *burden of proof.*

The **Affirmative** in its first speech (*at first glance*) needs to establish each one of the "**Basic Issues**" and therefore **meet its burden of proof**. To do this, the **Affirmative** should provide enough resolutional analysis that the audience and the other team would see just how the affirmative case fits under the resolution. (**Topicality**)

Next, the **Affirmative** should establish the problem that needs to be changed. (**Harm**) and show the causes of that problem. (**Inherency**) The **Affirmative** will need to present a **plan** (policy) that will solve the problem. After presenting the plan, the **Affirmative** can then show just how the plan will actually eliminate the problems. (**Solvency**) Solving the harms will produce advantages (**Significance**) that completes the justification of the affirmative proposal.

After the affirmative has proved (**burden of proof**) there is merit in the change proposed (**justification**), the affirmative must, *third*, **provide a policy to make that change (plan)**. The **plan** that the affirmative presents must be **workable** and **solve for the harms** presented and thus, provides **the advantages** claimed. In this way the affirmative can offer the judge a <u>decision calculus</u> (way to decide) that shows that it will be more beneficial to adopt the change (plan) than to continue without the change.

Affirmative's Basic Obligations

1. **Justify** the change from the status quo (harm, significance, inherency).

2. **Meet burden of proof** by proving that the justification for a change and the plan to solve for the harms is prima facie.

3. **Provide a plan** (solution to the harms) that works and solves.

These obligations are met by presenting arguments supporting each **core issue**, and it really doesn't matter the order in which you present the "**core issues.**" There are many formats for presenting an *<u>Affirmative Case</u>*. The important thing is that regardless of order or format **all the core issues are addressed**, and that the arguments that support them have enough evidence and analysis that **the truth within them is clear to the audience.**

Policy Debate—Affirmative Case Structure (Comparative Advantage)

Policy debate in its early beginnings required 100% solvency from the affirmative. As topic areas became larger, solving 100% of the problem became next to impossible. Therefore, the comparative advantage approach gained popularity and remains the preferred format today.

In terms of **solvency, the issue is tied to significance and therefore justification.** If a team can convince the judge that 1% solvency is significant enough to outweigh the negative disadvantage, then the case is justified regardless of structure. The whole premise of a comparative advantages case is that only enough advantage has to be gained to outweigh the arguments of the negative, specifically the disadvantages. This structure forces a decision calculus that compares advantages to disadvantages or risk to benefit.

In a comparative advantage case the affirmative must present a feasible and workable plan that will accrue advantages significant enough to justify the passage of plan. All the basic issues must be present within the structure. There are many comparative advantage formats, but the one below works well.

I. Introduction
II. Observation I – Harm
    a. Overview of the problem
    b. The significance of the problem
III. Observation II -- Inherency
    a. Cause of Problem
    b. Specific reason the problem hasn't been fixed
IV. Plan
    a. Mandates—Specific details of plan
    b. Funding
    c. Administration
    d. Enforcement
    e. Qualifiers (intent, final say on interpretation, etc.) (This may be done in narrative for or in outline form.)
V. Solvency/Advantage
    a. Harm
        i. Specific impact of harm (dead bodies)
        ii. Significance of harm (numbers)
    b. Uniqueness – The plan should be the best option to solve.
    c. Solvency
        i. Quote advocates that say plan will work or give examples of where plan has worked in other jurisdictions.
        ii. Visualize what it will be like post plan.
VI. Conclusion

Parliamentary Debate – Policy Resolution – Affirmative case

I. Introduction
II. Contention 1 – Resolution Analysis
    a. Definition of terms
    b. Resolution Analysis – policy, value, fact
    c. Criteria – net benefits or Comparative advantage
III. Contention II – Harm
IV. Contention III – Inherency
V. Plan
VI. Contention IV -- Solvency
VII. Advantage 1
VIII. Advantage 2
IX. Conclusion

Claims that one particular structure is not acceptable should be viewed in relationship to the presence of basic issues. If the basic issues are present, the structure is valid.

The Negative

The **Negative** is against the affirmative policy. The negative has no idea what the affirmative plan will be. The negative can only presume the resolution and research accordingly. That is why the negative will run **topicality** against an affirmative case that stretches the boundaries of the resolution.

Likewise, the affirmative won't know the negative case either. Before the negative even speaks, the debate **presumes** the status quo. The **presumption** is that the present situation is better than the unknown. If the negative defends the status quo and if the affirmative fails to meet their burden of proof, it is **presumed** that the negative wins the debate.

One of the **basic obligations of the Negative** is to provide *basic clash*. That means that they must provide arguments that directly oppose the affirmative claims. The **Negative** doesn't want the resolution adopted. So, the **Negative** must take exception to the major premises of the **Affirmative** case.

In modern debate, a second burden has been added, at least in practice. It is the **Burden to provide an alternative**. That burden could be met by presenting another plan (counter plan) or by showing that the status quo is a better alternative to solving the harms presented. Other positions are available to establish alternatives, but they are more theoretically based and are less used in practice.

Negative's Basic Obligations
1. Basic Clash—Dejustify.
2. **Provide an Alternative**—Status Quo or Counter Plan

Negative Strategies
The negative can use an assortment of strategies to provide basic clash at both the justification and solvency levels. In

challenging the justification of the affirmative proposal, the negative may choose a strategy to argue that there is no significant justification or at least very little reason for adopting the affirmative plan. This is called negation theory. It offers no alternative to the affirmative plan, but instead claims that the affirmative position is so bad we shouldn't consider it.

The negative can argue that the harms presented do not exist, or that some harm exists but to a lesser extent than the affirmative claims. People do not like change unless it is justified so there is no reason to adopt the Affirmative policy. This shows that the **advantages** received from adopting the plan have little or no **justification**. By itself this is a weak argument.

The negative may also choose a **strategy to argue against the solvency of the plan**. In every round of debate, the negative should run a disadvantage as part of the *solvency* strategy. Other *solvency* arguments would also help. This allows the negative to have some offence in weighing advantages versus disadvantages. By reducing the significance of the advantage, it will be easier for a disadvantage to outweigh the advantage. This strategy also does not offer an alternative, but is a stronger position than the previous strategy.

Another justification strategy is to clash with the harms and show how the status quo is solving the problem. The negative can claim that the present system **(status quo) is a better alternative than the affirmative plan**. The negative would point out **existing programs** that are helping solve the problem. The negative would also point out all the **negative consequences**

(*unique disadvantages*) that would come from adopting the affirmative plan. Then the negative would weigh the benefits of the status quo against the negative consequences of the plan (**decision calculus**). This is called a *progressive status quo* position and works when combined with *solvency* arguments to show that the status quo is a better plan for the harms than the affirmative.

As we said earlier, when the negative defends the status quo, they get **presumption**. Presumption is the basis of the phrase used in court that a person is innocent until proven guilty. It is the presumption of innocence. In debate it means that if all things are equal, we will prefer the status quo. It really is a matter of risk analysis. It is presumed that the status quo is less risky than a new policy unless proven differently. In other words, ties go to the negative.

The negative should form a **negative overview** that lays out their *strategy*. The affirmative has an affirmative case that they have formed around their proposed plan (policy). Every argument in the debate by the affirmative team is designed to support that case. Very often the negative will just **shoot from the hip**, each speaker simply making the arguments that they think will work.

Often, this **results in contradictions and weak argumentation**. Instead, it is important for the negative to come up with a **negative case** (negative overview or position) that combines all of their arguments into a unified coherent presentation. The negative does this by putting together the *strategy* or *strategies* they want to use and then presenting those strategies around their particular negative view of the debate. In debate, we often call that **"telling your story."** The negative should tell their story in every speech.

SPEECH ORDER

There are three sets of four speeches in a debate. The **first set of speeches** are called **constructive speeches**. The purpose of constructive speeches is to establish the arguments to be considered for each of the basic issues (harm, significance, inherency, and solvency). These speeches construct arguments that prove the need for the affirmative policy.

The **second set of speeches** are the **cross examination speeches**. Cross examination speeches follow each constructive speech in most formats. The purpose of the cross examination speech is to clarify just what the other team's arguments are and to establish ground for some argumentation of your own. The cross examination speeches take the form of questions and answers.

Many times students during cross examination will spend so much of their time trying to "catch" the other person in an inconsistency or in just being adversarial that they waste the entire allotment of time.

Cross examination is a speech and if used wisely, it can clarify and advance your arguments. Keep in mind that most judges will not flow (take notes) your cross examination. It may then be necessary, if an important argument presents itself, to bring the argument up in another speech.

The **third set of speeches** are the **rebuttal speeches**. The rebuttal speech is used to extend and rebuild arguments, refute the opposing team's arguments, and establish the core issues, and to **"tell your story."**

Policy Debate Speech Order & Times

1st Affirmative Constructive	8 Min.
2nd Negative Cross Examination	3 Min.
1st Negative Constructive	8 Min.
1st Affirmative Cross Examination	3 Min.
2nd Affirmative Constructive	8 Min.
1st Negative Cross Examination	3 Min.
2nd Negative Constructive	8 Min.
2nd Affirmative Cross Examination	3 Min.
1st Negative Rebuttal	5 Min.
1st Affirmative Rebuttal	5 Min.
2nd Negative Rebuttal	5 Min.
2nd Affirmative Rebuttal	5 Min.

Question: Each team receives an advantage because of the speaking order. Can you look at the order of the speeches above and figure out the advantage for the affirmative and the advantage for the negative? If you figure it out, share it with someone. I'll give you the answer later.

Presenting a General Argument

An argument is presented in a pattern or a structure. You will need to identify the issue being argued. You will need to state your claim, and present data (evidence supporting claim). You will then need to provide some analysis of that evidence to show how it warrants your claim. Finally, you will need to communicate the importance of your argument in relation to the audience. We call this impacting an argument.

Generic Argument Structure
1. State the issue being argued
    a. State your Claim (Conclusion)
    b. Give data (evidence supporting claim)
    c. Give warrant (analysis)
    d. Present an impact

Some Final Thoughts!

This has been a first look at **"Introduction to Policy Debate"** from a "Nuts and Bolts" point of view. The next chapter offers some in depth explanation of these basic concepts and a look at some more advanced arguments. As you gain experience in debate, you will want to revisit this chapter. Only after you have *experienced* this "<u>contest of argumentation</u>" will you be able to see the significance of all that you have just read. That is most true for the more abstract issues (theory) discussed in this chapter.

It is important that you not become discouraged. You will be receiving a lot of information that might not make a lot of sense at this time. Hang in there! The more you are exposed to debate and actually start making arguments, the more it will become clear.

Answer:

> The affirmative's advantage comes from having the first and last speech. The negative advantage comes from having two speeches back to back, 2nd Negative Constructive and 1st Negative Rebuttal. Only the 2nd Affirmative cross examination separates them. This is called the negative block.

These advantages set up a lot of strategies that strengthen each side's position. As you continue your exploration into debating, be on the look-out for how each of these advantages can be used to help your argumentation.

CHAPTER SIX
Advanced Theory: a Deeper Understanding

An Overview

Lesson Objective:
After completing this chapter a student should be able to:

1. Determine the difference between on and off case arguments

2. Ascertain the types of impact analysis

3. Distinguish between effects topicality and extra topicality

4. Identify the requirements of a counterplan

5. Correctly assess the validity of a kritik as well as identify the different types

New Terms:

on case	brink	magnitude	permutation
off case	impact	probability	internal link
uniqueness	topicality	effects	timeframe
link	kritik	decision calculus	
linear disadvantage		extra topicality	

Case/Off-Case Debate

In a traditional, competitive, academic debate setting, viewed through the lens of net benefit analysis, most argumentation will center on case side and/or off case debate. **Case side debate** would typically be focused on issues such as harms and solvency, whereas **off case debate** would be an examination of disadvantages and/or kritiks.

Many debaters neglect case side debate, arguing that such arguments are not offensive, or will not allow them to win with those arguments alone. Whether you chose to attack harms and/or solvency, it is critical to understand how such attacks could function in the context of a debate. The utility of such attacks is evidenced when run in conjunction with off case attacks such as a disadvantage.

The purpose of attacking harms and/or solvency is to mitigate, or weaken the justification for affirmative action as well as to call into question the ability of the affirmative plan to overcome, or solve for the harms they claim. If the negative team can weaken harms and/or solvency, the size/scope of the affirmative advantages are reciprocally reduced, thus making it that much easier for the negative off case positions to outweigh the affirmative.

DISADVANTAGES

Perhaps the most common off case argument is the **disadvantage**. As discussed in Chapter Five, a disadvantage is merely a discussion of the negative side effects that stem from the action suggested by the affirmative. Disadvantages are generally structured in the following fashion.

1. **Uniqueness** – shows how the status quo is acting in the manner suggest by the affirmative plan, and as a result, cannot be causing the same type of impact.
2. **Link** – broad statement of how affirmative action initially connects or moves towards a negative consequence
3. **Internal Link** – a more precise, specific statement, often providing exact analysis, explicitly providing empirical evidence of how such action causes a move toward the eventual impact
4. **Brink** – the point at which there is no return (the edge of the cliff) – when the affirmative action will precisely trigger the impact

5. **Impact** – overt statement of the negative side effect of the affirmative plan

One variation on the disadvantage would be what is oft referred to as a **linear disadvantage**. The linear disadvantage follows the previously mentioned structure, with the exception of skipping the uniqueness level. Suffice to say, such a disadvantage would argue that the link, brink and impact are already occurring in the status quo. This means that the only impact would be what is furthered or amplified as a result of the affirmative plan, creating a larger impact than the one created by the status quo.

Most negative teams will suggest that the round be evaluated through the net benefit lens, and will ultimately offer some sort of **impact calculus**, or manner of determining if the disadvantage outweighs the affirmative advantages.

Frequently, impact calculus is comprised of three parts:

> **Timeframe** - Evaluates how soon the impacts would occur. Specifically address each impact against each other in an effort to determine which impacts occur first.
>
> **Magnitude** - Magnitude looks at how big the impacts are. For example, nuclear war versus quality of life.
>
> **Probability** - This is a way to examine different impacts in comparison to one another and determine just how likely each one is to occur. Winning on probability does not always win an impact debate, but it is an important

aspect of weighing the issue. This portion should also be used to beg the question of which team has more evidence and warrants for their claim.

COUNTERPLANS

Many of the advanced arguments in debate may be perceived as highly technical, often referred to as theory arguments. However, upon closer examination, most of these arguments are grounded in the practical world. Perhaps no argument is a clearer example than the counterplan.

A counterplan is usually an alternative approach (plan) being presented by the negative team in an effort to achieve the same effect (advantages) as the affirmative plan without certain undesirable negative consequences (disadvantages).

A counterplan agrees with the affirmative that there is justification for a change in the present system. The negative team then rejects the status quo, rejects the affirmative proposal, and proposes a different plan to solve for the justification. The debate then centers on who has the best plan.

People propose counter plans in real life all the time. Example: Jim says he is hungry (justification) and proposes we all go to McDonald's to eat (plan). Ralph is hungry too (he agrees with the justification), but he proposes we order pizza from Pizza Hut (counter plan).

Traditionally a counterplan had 3 basic requirements that need to be met before the counterplan is worthy of consideration or competitive with the affirmative. The requirements are:

Non-Topical – the counterplan needs to fall outside of the boundaries of the resolution, thus ensuring that if the judge were to find the plan desirable they could vote negative without supporting the resolution. The affirmative team is to be the only side upholding the resolution. Whereas if the counterplan were topical, a vote in its favor could also be seen as a vote for the resolution.

Net Beneficial – simply coming up with an alternative plan isn't enough, the negative team must demonstrate that their idea is advantageous. For example:

- Affirmative Plan: The United States will pull all of its troops out of Iraq immediately.

    Advantage of Affirmative Plan: Troops are overworked, under-paid, and have had lengthy deployments, all of which have led to diminished moral and readiness. They need a break, and the best way to do that is bring the troops home immediately.

- Negative Counterplan: The United States will pull all of its troops out of Iraq over the next 18 months.

    Negative Counterplan is Net Beneficial as bringing troops home as fast as possible is dangerous as we would be unable to coordinate security as we were leaving; it would just be a chaotic mass exodus. The troops and Iraqi civilians would not be safe without proper coordination of the exit. The counterplan allows the troops to return home at a rate that will not jeopardizing their safety.

Mutually Exclusive – The counterplan and the plan cannot operate in the same space and/or at the same time as they would exclude one another. Thus only one of the options could be selected. As shown in the previous example, the counterplan is mutually exculsive as it is not possible to bring the troops home immediately (as affirmative desired) and bring them home in 18 months (as per the negative counterplan. Thus the counterplan is mutually exclusive.

In arguing against a counterplan, the affirmative should always look to determine if the counterplan is non-topical, has a net benefit and is mutually exclusive. If not, this is at least a starting point for arguing why the counterplan should not be considered as option over the affirmative plan. However, most well-conceived counterplans will at least initially meet these standards.

Most judges will make their decision of whether to vote for the affirmative plan or the negative counterplan on the basis of the greatest benefit. As a result, it would be wise of the affirmative to "take on the role of the negative" in a sense, possibly running a disadvantage to the negative counterplan, or at the very least trying to show how the affirmative plan is ultimately most desirable. A typical negative strategy would be to run a counterplan in conjunction with a disadvantage and perhaps solvency mitigation (arguments which weaken the overall claims that the affirmative plan can solve) thus trying to show how the counterplan is more desirable since it doesn't have the disadvantage or the lack of overall solvency that they are claiming is the issue with the affirmative.

Perhaps the most common argument presented against a counterplan is a permutation, often referred to as a perm. A perm is simply a test of competition to determine if the counterplan is truly a viable option, to the exclusion of the affirmative plan. A perm simply tests whether the negative counterplan and an affirmative plan can operate together. Common perms include:

1. Do both (affirmative plan and negative counterplan at the same time)
2. Do Affirmative plan and then the negative counterplan
3. Do negative counterplan and then the affirmative plan

If any of the above options are deemed viable or possible, then the judge has no reason to vote against the affirmative. When the affirmative perms the counterplan they are not shifting their advocacy, but merely offering a hypothetical scenario which demonstrates that the negative counterplan is not a competitive option when compared to the affirmative plan.

In addition to offering permutations to the counterplan the affirmative can also attack the counterplan as if it were another affirmative case, arguing that it has a solvency deficit or results in disadvantages that would not otherwise have occurred.

TOPICALITY

While topicality in its purest form has been discussed previously (Chapter 5) there are still a few subtle variations which one should understand. As was discussed previously, topicality is a common procedural argument used to frame the round or determine the ground for each side. In terms of how that is actually put into practice, it follows the same set up as other procedural arguments: Interpretation/Definition, Violation, Reasons to Prefer/Standards, and Voters.

Below is an example of a word that is commonly used in resolutions – Increase.

- A. DEFINITION – Increase – to become larger or greater in size.

- B. VIOLATION – The affirmative team does not increase anything in their plan, they remove a policy.

- C. REASONS TO PREFER or STANDARDS –

    1. Limits – Putting limits on the topic is preferable because without them the affirmative team could do anything they want and the negative team would have no way to predict it.

2. Predictability – Definitions that are not predictable reduce the fairness and clash in round.

D. VOTERS or reasons why topicality should be voted upon

1. A Priori - In Latin, a priori literally means "prior to." In the context of debate, an a priori argument means that the judge should evaluate the argument prior to evaluating any other argument in the round. The reason for this is simple. The affirmative team has the advantage of creating and advocating a plan in the debate round. If the affirmative did not have any parameters limiting what the plan could resolve, the affirmative would always win simply by creating a plan that is wildly unpredictable by any negative team.

2. Competitive Equity or Education – It is only fair that the negative team be afforded the opportunity to examine the limitations of the resolution, calling for the judge to examine whether said boundaries have been violated by the affirmative team. If so, this would creative a competitive imbalance, being unfair to the negative team.

There are many different standards and voters that can be used when creating topicality shells. Standards include (but are not limited to):

- ***Brightline*** – measures how clear the division is between topical and non-topical cases under a certain interpretation

- **Common Person** — interpretation is what would be most expected should they inquire of a "person on the street"

- **Predictability** — (defined above under standards)

- **Grammar** — interpretation most closely follows or adheres to conventional grammatical meaning, accounting for parts of speech

- **Ground** — interpretation provides ample space (ground) for each side to defend

- **Limits** — (defined above under standards)

Voters:

- **Jurisdiction** — as per a court of law, if a judge has a limit scope or filed which he or she can examine, the case may be thrown out of court without it merits being examined; similarly, if an affirmative case is non-topical, the judge must vote negative regardless of any benefits.

- **A-Priori** — (defined above under voters)

- **Competitive Equity or Education** — (defined above under voters)

- **Fairness** — There must be roughly equal ground for strategy between affirmative and negative teams. One team having an advantage is grounds to be voted against.

- **Competitive Equity** – (defined above under voters)

Beyond the tradition topicality attack lie the equally effective yet lesser heard arguments of 1) effects topicality and 2) extra topicality. The overall structure of these arguments is no different than described above, although the initial premise is distinct.

While topicality argues that the entirety of the affirmative plan and case lie outside the bounds of the resolution, effects topicality is a subset which argues that the plan text of the affirmative is non topical and that the only way the affirmative is able to achieve even a portion of the topic is through its effects.

Traditionalists will argue that to determine whether an affirmative is topical is to examine the "plan in a vacuum." This very test would typically be sufficient to prove that the plan is topical only through the effects of the plan and hence is non topical.

Extra topicality differs in that the negative would be arguing that the affirmative has gone beyond the scope of the resolution. If a resolution called for the affirmative to improve the economy of the great plains states, yet the affirmative enacted a plan that improved the economy of the nation as a whole, the negative team would claim the affirmative is extra topical.

Being extra topical gives the affirmative a distinct advantage as they negative would be forced to argue outside of the subject area they anticipated. While a traditional topicality attack would argue the affirmative selected a case outside of the resolution, a charge of extra topicality suggests the affirmative is not only covering the boundaries of the resolution, but moving beyond them as well.

KRITIKS

Another commonly used advanced theory argument is the kritik. The kritik stems largely from the German philosophers Georg Wilhelm Friedrich Hegel and Martin Heidegger. The use of this argument is continually evolving and as a result, is often poorly understood by many judges and unfortunately debaters as well.

"Kritik" is the German word for the English "critique," and both words are pronounced the same way. Debaters are already familiar with the term "critique" as it is commonly used to describe the oral and/or written commentary that judges offer teams following the round; however when referencing the argument, the German spelling (kritik) is typically used.

Kritiks are arguments which question the underlying assumptions imbedded in the arguments, values, presentation style or language choices made in the debate. Typically, the kritik is used as a tool for the negative team against the affirmative but it is increasingly being used by affirmative teams as well.

Kritiks typically have five characteristics:

1. The kritik questions the fundamental assumptions of the round. It looks at issues lurking within the presentation style or language choices of their opponents, rather than taking the presentation at its face value. The result of this is that the debate shifts away from policy discussion, often toward discussing questions of fact or value.

2. The kritik is usually presented as an absolute argument. It demands a yes-or-no response from the judge, rather than an impact to be weighed against other arguments. The team that introduces such an argument will be arguing in the pre-fiat realm, prior to the illusory magic wand which enables affirmatives access to their advantages. Such an argument suggest that the damage inflicted by the opposition's use of language, methodology for round evaluation or implicitly or explicitly held values perpetuate negative impacts, occurring as soon as those choices were made. Thus the opposition should not be able to attempt to outweigh the damage by examining the benefits or advantages which stem from their positions. Ultimately the team running the kritik would argue that advantages that are argued in the debate are theoretical and merely a by-product of the game we are playing, whereas the choices of language or values have a real impact on those present in the debate round.

3. The kritik may be non-unique. The side presenting a kritik can make the same assumptions for which it is

kritiking the opposing team. They will argue that the choices were first made by their opponents and as a result can only serve as a loss for the opposing team.

4. Kritiks are non-comparative. The kritiks questions and objects, but does not always offer an alternative. At most, kritiks suggest a vague alternatives, but do not usually specify which one should be selected. A "kritik of capitalism," for instance, may suggest that capitalism be rejected, and the affirmative's capitalistic underpinnings should be rejected as well. But the negative presenting the argument would not be required to select a precise alternative to capitalism, such as fascism or socialism.

5. Kritiks are a priori voting issues. Since they represent fundamental considerations on which presentations are built, they demand to be evaluated before substantive issues such as inherency, topicality, or disadvantages are considered. If the basis of those arguments is faulty, as the kritik suggests, then we should discard the arguments without further examination.

As kritiks are generic arguments, they often seem to ignore the details presented by the opposition, rather focusing on the core reasons underlying the opposing case, style and diction of the presentation, or the manner in which a team wants the round evaluated.

Most typically, there are 3 types of kritiks:

1. **Language** - The language kritik examines the choice of words made by the opposition, whether words they freely spoke or simply read from a piece of evidence. For instance, should the vocabulary of the opposition include a racist or sexist term, they could be called out for perpetrating what would ultimately be considered a dehumanizing view of a particular group. The link to the kritik is merely the fact that specific choices were made to use language that is deemed offensive.

2. **Value** - The value kritik is probably the most common criticism, typically run to expose the ongoing negative consequences of the value(s) the opposition is upholding, whether implicitly or explicitly. For example, if an affirmative plan included an advantage of furthering United States economic growth, the negative could offer a critique questioning the bastion of capitalism, pointing out all of the ongoing ills that capitalism spreads throughout contemporary American society. The kritik would demonstrate that the affirmative plan further entrenches capitalism and further heightens the damage of such a system.

3. **Methodological** - The methodological kritik questions the manner in which a given team wants the round evaluated; in other words, the weighing mechanism is called into question. Thus if your opponent suggested that the round be evaluated through a utilitarian (greatest good for the greatest number) lens, such a lens or framework could allow for outright majority rule

and oppression of any/all minority groups or their points of view.

In attacking a kritik, there are a number of potential arguments which can be offered against almost any kritik. (Please note that these arguments should not all be used in conjunction, as some combinations may be contradictory)

I. Kritiks are logically flawed

A. Kritiks are infinitely regressive – a kritik is constantly questioning the value or importance of a particular stance, a question which can again be posed no matter the response to the initial question.

B. Not all assumptions should be examined – at some point we need to draw a line in the sand and suggest that this is as far as we will go – we have reached a breaking point, or a point at which we will take a definitive stand.

C. Not a black and white issue – controversial assumptions are not simply true or false – they are more or less plausible.

D. Kritik bites itself – Kritiks question the underlying assumptions behind a given claim, yet if we extrapolate this objective, we should also question the underlying assumption(s) behind the kritik itself.

E. Deconstruction is counterproductive – continuously breaking down every statement to uncover the inherent meaning or determine the implicit values undermines the meaning of the activity of debate. We are to evaluate each team in reference to their stance on the resolution, not on the merits of ideas are at best tangential.

II. Policy
   A. All arguments must function within the policy framework – the subject matter of debate is public policy. The resolution is always a question of policy. Debate has been defined for decades as policy centered because it always selects a question of policy.

   B. Policy debate is preferred - the subject matter of debate is public policy. The resolution is always a question of policy. Debate has been defined for decades as policy centered because it always selects question of policy.

   C. Action and struggle should precede critical analysis – Philosopher Paulo Freire argued that a struggle against dominant ideas first requires a concrete starting that is shown through acts of resistance. Once the acts have occurred, only then can oppositional ideologies be developed.

III. Alternative
   A. Abusiveness – If the affirmative team is to be responsible for ending the atrocities of the kritik and

negative team doesn't present an alternative (to do so), the best the judge can do is vote against the affirmative team, not for the negative team. This would void the concept of presumption because the negative team kritks the status quo and lacks an alternative.

B. Noncomparable arguments are inherently unpersuasive - all policies have some flaw. If all negative team needed to do was point out a few flaws, they would always win. Constructive thought is as important as critical thought, because solving problems is more important that simply identifying them.

C. No alternative leaves a void – even a flawed theory is better than no theory at all. Without an alternative we have no cause to change our beliefs.

IV. Ballot is not key – discourse and in-round implications fail

A. No influence - due to the competitive nature of debate, the ideas behind the kritik are reduced to "just another argument." The argument is viewed hypothetically which means the ideas in the kritik don't actually change the participants in this round. The only real world impacts of debate rounds is competition. Debaters don't make real decisions in round and while in rounds are not in positions of influence.

B. Reality shapes discourse - not the other way around. Languages around the world prove that reality shapes discourse. Because reality can be different for everyone in the round, assessing an issue in the round does not guarantee that we'll find the truth, assuming such a thing even exists. Thus even if we come to an agreement regarding the kritik, it plays no role in shaping us outside of the round of competition.

C. Voting affirmative doesn't stop rethinking - The judge and the debaters can continue to ponder the kritik even after the round ends. The judge can always reserve the right to change their mind as related to the concepts in the kritik, independent of their decision for who wins/loses the round.

D. Discourse solves theory is flawed - If language does create reality, then different cultures with different languages would have different realities. If that were true, then cross-cultural communication would be difficult if not impossible. As we know such communication is possible, it proves that talk alone does not alter reality.

V. *Educational Value*

A. The marketplace of ideas is structurally incapable of finding the truth – Professor of Law, Benjamin Duval Jr. argues "They implicitly assume that if the market operated at peak efficiency, truth would be discovered, and suggest only that there exists a partial disequilibrium which renders the market temporarily incapable of correctly tabulating the results of free debates. Answers to these attacks have not been offered, but the answers, like the questions, do not go to the core of the problem."

B. Relevancy is relevant - the ideas in the kritik are not relevant to the topic, thus legitimizing ad hominem attacks and other arguments that do not directly link to the presented ideas.

C. Rejecting the kritik is not intellectually intolerant — Critical thinking skills allow anyone to gather, process and evaluation information. We make choices and decisions every day. There is no reason why one more will push us over the brink.

D. Time — The time constraints faced be each team in a debate preclude honest, in depth evaluation. Attempting to evaluate such deep philosophical concepts in a matter of a few minutes does no service to the present concepts or their framers. These constraints can lead to over simplification and rash decision making. A true examination of the merits of the kritik should take place outside of the competitive arena as there is unlimited time for such an examination.

E. Increased mental stagnation — Similar kritiks have been argument for years in competitive debate. Their continued use as an argument to win a round leads to desensitization of what should be significant issues, thus completely contrary to the goals of the team presenting the argument.

VI. Fiat

A. Fiat is not utopian - To endorse or reject the desirability of a plan is not utopian. We engage in this process of opinion formation every time we make a decision.

B. Uniqueness is important – As the kritik is a non-unique argument, typically occurring in the status quo, the impacts are felt whether or not the affirmative plan is rejected. Since the affirmative plan is not uniquely responsible for the impacts of the kritik, there is no reason to reject the affirmative team.

C. Must have theory before practice – It is preferable to allow the affirmative team to examine the outcome/benefits/advantages of the affirmative plan via fiat, as it allows us to test ideas. It is logical to assume the plan will be implemented before we can examine the desirability of the plan.

This chapter was not meant to offer a comprehensive listing of all advanced arguments, but merely to discuss those which are commonly heard. The arguments presented are simply a starting point, as there is no limit to the types of arguments which can be presented during a debate.

CHAPTER SEVEN
Applied Argumentation

An Overview

New Terms:

Tournament Model	Rounds	CEDA
National Debate Tournament		Meta-Debate
Lincoln Douglas	NDT	NSDA
Public Forum	NFA	NPDA
Leadership	NPTE	IPDA

The world we live in is one of arguments. Throughout this book you have encountered a variety of perspectives about types of propositions and both basic and advanced techniques for engaging in argumentation. In this chapter we will explore just a few of the many ways you will find yourself applying the concepts we have discussed so far.

Academic Debate

Since the early eighteenth century students who were fortunate enough to attend universities have had the benefit of a curriculum that included instruction in rhetoric. Beginning in the early twentieth century a number of prestigious universities in the United States began to sponsor competitive debates between students representing their various institutions.

These events were often day-long competitions featuring a team from each school debating a previously-agreed-upon proposition. Prior to World War II this model of competition grew in popularity. The resource rationing and travel restrictions that came as a result of World War II forced tremendous changes in the way competitive debating was done. One such change was the implementation of the **tournament model.**

Instead of only two schools engaging in a debate that was several hours long, the tournament model allowed teams or individuals from multiple schools to engage in a multiple debates or **rounds** of competition. This proved to be a highly efficient method for maximizing the educational benefits and competitive opportunities of academic debate. The tournament model proved so popular with educators and students that it persists up until the present day.

One of the earliest tournaments was the **National Debate Tournament.** There had been a National Debate Tournament topic since 1920. In 1947 the U.S. Military Academy at West Point assumed responsibility for the National Debate

Tournament from 1947 until 1967 when the American Forensic Association began to host the National Debate Tournament. From 1920 until 1971 the NDT was essentially the only national debate tournament and therefore established norms for all college debaters across the U.S.

One effect of this was that **NDT** debates (starting the early 1960s) began to become much faster and more technical. These developments, which were driven by competition, began to make competitive intercollegiate debating less accessible to new students. In 1971 the Cross Examination Debate Association (**CEDA**) established a new format of debate designed to be a more accessible alternative to NDT.

In the ensuing years, CEDA debaters began to adopt the practices of NDT debaters until the two organizations formally merged in 1996.

NDT/CEDA Debate

As a format of academic debate, NDT/CEDA exists today as an extremely fast and technical format of policy debate. This remains the standard format of an NDT/CEDA round:

First Affirmative Constructive	9 Min.
Cross Examination	3 Min.
First Negative Constructive	9 Min.
Cross Examination	3 Min.

Second Affirmative Constructive	9 Min.
Cross Examination	3 Min.
Second Negative Constructive	9 Min.
Cross Examination	3 Min.
First Negative Rebuttal	6 Min.
First Affirmative Rebuttal	6 Min.
Second Negative Rebuttal	6 Min.
Second Affirmative Rebuttal	6 Min.

Prep Time: 10 minutes per team

NDT/CEDA debaters consider themselves to be among the most elite of all college debaters because of the degree to which they engage in **meta-debate**. Meta-debate is the process of critically evaluating the practices, norms, and culture of the activity of debate while simultaneously participating in it.

For instance, a typical NDT/CEDA round will likely feature kritiks, performance affirmatives, and a dizzying array of advanced argumentation techniques that simultaneously critique the activity while participating in it.

Of course, even in a format such as this, that often prides itself on being "real debate" because it is exclusively policy, there is still a good bit of implicit and explicit value and fact argumentation to be heard. For instance, a performance affirmative wherein the affirmative team reads poetry describing the harsh realities of urban poverty rather than presenting a topical plan, will often do so inspired by the idea that such a performance is more important than a more standard form of policy advocacy—thus perhaps affirming the value of social justice.

NATIONAL SPEECH AND DEBATE ASSOCIATION LINCOLN DOUGLAS DEBATE (HIGH SCHOOL)

As with college debate, early high school debate was dominated by policy. However, in the 1980s students and coaches began to demand an alternative to traditional policy debate. So the National Forensic League (now the National Speech and Debate Association) began sanctioning a new format known as Lincoln Douglas debate.

It was very different from traditional policy since it emphasized values and value-centered argumentation. Resolutions dealt with value conflicts and moral obligations embedded within domestic political issues, foreign relations, and the general tension often extant between individual rights and the rights and obligations of the larger society.

The format was named in honor of the celebrated debates between Abraham Lincoln and Frederick Douglas in the 1858 U.S. Senate race in Illinois. This format continues to thrive in high school forensics competitions. The format looks like this:

Affirmative Constructive	6 Min.
Cross Examination	3 Min.
Negative Constructive	7 Min.
Cross Examination	3 Min.
First Affirmative Rebuttal	4 Min.
Negative Rebuttal	6 Min.
Second Affirmative Rebuttal	3 Min.

Prep Time: 5 minutes per debater

NFA Lincoln Douglas Debate

In 1990 the National Forensics Association (**NFA**) began offering competition in Lincoln Douglas debate. Lincoln Douglas exists as a one-on-one format that (in its current formulation) is also exclusively policy in its orientation. In contemporary competitions, Lincoln Douglas speeches are often delivered in a rapid-fire fashion.

This is ironic since this format was originally conceived as a more conversational alternative to the faster and less audience-oriented NDT/CEDA debate. NFA Lincoln Douglas debates use the following format:

Affirmative Constructive	6 Min.
Cross Examination	3 Min.

Negative Constructive	7 Min.
Cross Examination	3 Min.
First Affirmative Rebuttal	6 Min.
Negative Rebuttal	6 Min.
Second Affirmative Rebuttal	3 Min.

Prep Time: 4 minutes per debater

Contemporary NFA LD is generally fast-paced and places major emphasis upon features of policy debate including large-scale impacts such nuclear war, mass extinction, dehumanization and the like. The focus upon impacts and impact calculus likely stems from the fact that NFA LD prescribes a judging paradigm based exclusively upon the classic policy stock issues (Harms, Inherency, Topicality, Solvency, and Significance).

NPDA/NPTE Parliamentary Debate

In the early 1990s the **National Parliamentary Debate Association** was created. Parliamentary debate took collegiate team debate competition in several innovative directions. Two features of parliamentary debate were particularly striking. First, there was no annual topic.

Indeed, the topics for each round varied from round to round and were only announced 15 minutes prior to the start of the debate. The second innovate feature of parliamentary debate was its prohibition on quoting, reading, or using directly-cited evidence. The use of evidence (a necessary feature in every other format of debate) was prohibited in this format and replaced by a "common knowledge" paradigm—often expressed as the maxim that the debaters were only allowed to directly reference evidence or statistics that were consistent with "what the well-read college student should know."

Both changes were instituted to encourage broad participation in the activity by a wide range of competitors regardless of their previous experience in debate. It was believed that a format that both prohibited specific evidence and information and encouraged debaters to debate a wide variety of topics would result in a format that was not only accessible to non-specialists but also engaging for debaters, judges, and audience members.

Early parliamentary debates were usually devoid of the various debate theory arguments that were so much a part of exclusively policy formats. This is the format of a parliamentary debate:

Prime Minister	7 Min.
Leader of Opposition	8 Min.
Member of Government	8 Min.
Member of Opposition	8 Min.

    Leader of Opposition Rebuttal   4 Min.

    Prime Minister Rebuttal   5 Min.

        Prep Time: 15-20 minutes pre-round prep time

Through the 1990s and the early decades of the 2000s, the format has evolved such that speed and spread are now common. In 2001, the **National Parliamentary Tournament of Excellence** began hosting a national tournament in addition to NPDA nationals. NPTE has encouraged such innovations in the format. Parliamentary debate remains a relatively popular format of debate that prizes innovation in college debate.

INTERNATIONAL PUBLIC DEBATE (COLLEGE)

In the mid-1990s the **International Public Debate Association** was formed to offer additional competitive opportunities for college debaters. IPDA or public debate is a one-on-one format of debate that features speeches that are slightly shorter than those in parliamentary debate. Like parliamentary, public debate does not have a standing topic and features pre-round preparation.

Unlike parliamentary, it encourages the use of reference materials as evidence. However, public debaters are not permitted to directly read extensive amounts of evidence. The current IPDA bylaws stipulate that evidence should be memorized or paraphrased for use in the round. The IPDA takes very seriously the ideal of broad competition and the ability of all to participate.

That is why IPDA debate has a number of divisions. Novice division is available to beginners who are either high school or university students. Varsity competition is available to more experienced competitors who are either high school or university students. These two formats are standard in most other formats of debate with the exception that the IPDA opens its competitions to high school students as well—IPDA is quite unique in this aspect.

IPDA also offers a "professional" division for those who have graduated from college, but still wish to participate. This is the format of a (one-on-one) IPDA round:

Affirmative	5 Min.
Cross Examination	2 Min.
Negative	6 Min.
Cross Examination	2 Min.
First Affirmative Rebuttal	3 Min.
Negative Rebuttal	5 Min.
Second Affirmative Rebuttal	3 Min.

Prep Time: 30 minutes pre-round prep (Generally no in-round prep time)

Although it began as a one-on-one format of debate, IPDA also sponsors competition in two-person team IPDA debate. That format is as follows:

Affirmative Constructive	4 Min.
Cross Examination	2 Min.
Negative Constructive	5 Min.
Cross Examination	2 Min.
Affirmative Constructive	5 Min.
Cross Examination	2 Min.
Negative Constructive	4 Min.
Negative Rebuttal	3 Min.
Affirmative Rebuttal	4 Min.
Negative Rebuttal	4 Min.
Affirmative Rebuttal	3 Min.

IPDA debate is particularly popular with students who are new to debate. It is quite popular in the South although programs from all across the U.S. participate in IPDA.

Public Forum Debate (High School & College)

In 2007, the National Forensic League (now the National Speech and Debate Association) began offering public forum debate. Unlike parliamentary debate, public forum is evidence-based and calls for debaters to make their arguments in the context of very concise speeches. It was initially compared to "crossfire" debate in honor of the once-popular CNN show of the same name.

Each month a new public forum topic is released and debated for the whole month—requiring debaters and coaches to stay abreast of many subjects. The topics debated in public forum vary widely and are generally policy-oriented.

Nevertheless, public forum debaters are encouraged not to debate the resolutions with a simply fact/value/policy frame alone, but to consider how the resolution itself and their arguments may involve a number of diverse perspectives.

For instance, in a debate about gender equity in American education, the debaters are invited to consider both the value and policy implications of the reforms that may be suggested as part of the debate. Public forum is unique in that there is no pre-determination of affirmative or negative for each round of competition.

Rather, the debaters meet together and flip a coin. The winner of the toss is entitled to decide if their team would rather select their speaking order (first or second) or the side they would prefer to take for the round (Public forum uses "Pro" to refer to the Affirmative and "Con" to refer to the Negative). Public forum has found a popular following among high school students. A high school public forum round typically consists of the following:

Team A:
    First Speaker: Constructive Speech   4 Min.

Team B:
    First Speaker: Constructive Speech   4 Min.

    Crossfire (between first speakers)   3 Min.

Team A:
    Second Speaker: Rebuttal   4 Min.

Team B:
    Second Speaker: Rebuttal   4 Min.

    Crossfire (between second speakers)   3 Min.

Team A:
    First Speaker: Summary   2 Min.

Team B:
    First Speaker: Summary   2 Min.

    Grand Crossfire (All speakers)   3 Min.

Team A:
    Second Speaker: Final Focus/Last Shot   2 Min.

Team B:
> Second Speaker: Final Focus/Last Shot   2 Min.

> Prep Time: 3 minutes per team

In 2012 public forum debate was offered as a collegiate debate event for the first time. Since then, its popularity with college debaters has grown steadily. College public forum is identical to its high school counterpart with the exception of two differences; there is no "grand crossfire" toward the end of the debate and college debaters are only allowed two minutes of preparation time.

This consideration of the dizzying array of competitive debate formats available to students demonstrates several things about the current state of academic debating in the U.S. First, there is tremendous diversity of competitive experiences available to students. (And this list is far from exhaustive.)

Second, academic debate is alive and well within the U.S. and throughout the world. The past two decades have witnessed the rise of more and more opportunities for teams from the U.S. to enter and compete in a host of international debate competitions.

Similarly, debaters from other nations around the world often organize and participate in tours of U.S. colleges and universities.

Uses of Argumentation

We hope this book has helped you become more familiar with the vast world of debate, a number of the techniques that will help you become a more effective debater, and provide you a sense of the ways that including debate as a part of your educational experience will be beneficial to you.

We will close this chapter by examining some of the ways that the–application of these techniques of argumentation will be most beneficial. Specifically, we argue that studying argumentation will better prepare you for success as a leader in your workplace and community while simultaneously making you a better globally-minded citizen.

We will begin by considering some of the skills that argumentation helps you to cultivate. Effective debating begins and ends with effective research. When preparing for a debate, the debater must become familiar with all aspects of the topic under consideration. You must not only seek out information, but it must be the best and most recent information.

The fact that academic debating occurs in a competitive environment means debaters will usually lose if their evidence is not of the highest caliber. Debaters must also seek out information that is as free as possible from overt ideological bias. The ability to do effective research of this type is tremendously helpful when it comes to preparing sales presentations, analyzing news reports in the popular press, and critically evaluating the claims of that salesperson who wants you to spend just a few more dollars to purchase the latest product. In short, quality research is both beneficial and essential.

Not only must you be a good researcher, you must be able to effectively (and often quickly) analyze what you find. Let's assume you are debating the policy merits of raising the minimum wage.

Naturally, this topic would generate a number of opinions and reports from official-sounding advocacy groups on both sides of this controversy. Training in debate gives students the opportunity to critically-investigate the details of how and why the sources they are using arrived at their conclusions.

Doing this causes the debater to apply and consider a host of important concepts, including random sampling, bias, reliability, statistical significance, and a great many others. This type of training in data analysis will serve you well in everything from using advanced statistics in graduate school to analyzing the methodologies of Consumer Reports and other publications that evaluate consumer products.

Skills Developed or Enhanced by Training in Argumentation

- Research
- Analysis of Data
- Speaking/Writing Skills
- Language Use/Word Economy
- Understanding Current Events
- Appealing to Decision Makers

- Emotional Intelligence
- Leadership
- Citizenship

Debate makes you a better speaker and writer. The verbal fluency that is necessary to win in debate (especially in formats that are audience-oriented) is a matter of constant polish and practice. New debaters learn very quickly that they must adopt effective public speaking behaviors such as effective eye contact, vocal variety, gestures that help to punctuate the verbal message, and how to avoid those annoying vocalized pauses (uums and eers that are often used as mere verbal fillers) to name just a few.

Likewise, students in debate become better writers. The constancy of writing practice that students receive in debate teaches them more about the mechanics of writing. They learn to write with the knowledge that their work is going to be critically evaluated by others—an understanding that makes one much more focused during the writing (and rewriting) process.

The attention to writing detail that is required for debaters to succeed at the highest levels makes them much more attractive for career positions that require effective and careful writing.

One of the first lessons that new debaters learn is that writing done merely to be read (as in the case of an essay or research paper) is far different from writing that one does in preparation for a speech or debate.

As the old saying goes, a speech is not merely an essay on hind legs. Debaters learn to write in the oral style—which is more conscious of word economy. This helps students learn to avoid redundancy in their writing and write with a type of crispness that will serve them well in their careers.

When establishing the structure of a debate constructive, debaters often find it necessary and desirable to give concise and clear names to the various contentions that they are using. In a debate about the merits of affirmative action, they may label their first contention "Economic Effects" rather than using the fully-articulated argument in order to label the whole contention.

They will save the full articulation to be developed as they dive into the details of the argument. This practice of writing with word economy in mind is very beneficial when it becomes necessary for them to summarize lengthy and detailed information later in their professional careers.

As should be evident from the wide variety of examples we have provided throughout this book, debate teaches you a great deal about the world. It is impossible to learn about the negative aspects of U.S. military intervention in other countries around the globe without learning much about the history of such efforts, the complex relationships that characterize global geopolitical affairs, and the questions about the military and economic feasibility of such efforts. In debate, you learn to be far more than simply a casual observer of political and global affairs. This not only makes you a better-rounded individual, but a deeply-informed citizen.

Since it is a competitive activity that involves "winning over" a judge or panel of judges, successful debaters become adept at learning how to tailor their arguments and appeals to a wide variety of judges who have the power to render decisions.

Debaters must adapt to the paradigms of a wide variety of judges. This skill is crucial to a host of professional behaviors—including getting a job.

Although it is often not articulated among the benefits of debate, debaters must learn to cultivate a strong emotional intelligence. Daniel Goleman argues that emotional intelligence is comprised of "self-awareness, self-regulation, motivation, empathy, and social skill . . ."[i]

Participation in debate demands that you think of others and not just yourself. Debaters must work well with others including their teammates, opponents, coaches, and their judges. Any debater who simply does and says what he or she wants to do with little regard to the thoughts and perspectives of others will not be successful.

As is also implicit in Goleman's articulation of emotional intelligence, debaters must be self-motivated and disciplined in order to achieve their objectives. They must drive themselves hard in order to be successful and must argue their positions against and in front of others in a way that invites rather than demands agreement. In this way, interscholastic debate is one of the best laboratories for the teaching and learning of leadership and leadership skills.

As mentioned earlier, argumentation skills are necessary for leadership. There are many theories of leadership and a wide range of ideas about what effective leaders do. We believe that **leadership is the act of clearly articulating a vision for a group or organization while simultaneously inviting group members to participate in the joys and challenges inherent to achieving a series of shared objectives.**

Given this formulation, it is obvious that communication plays a central role in leadership. In the contemporary business or organizational environment, leaders must not only be articulate they must be effectively articulate. They must be able to take the perspectives of others long enough to consider the potential objections that others may have to a proposed course of action and work collaboratively with them in order to surmount the obstacles that are before them.

They must accomplish all of this while summarizing and synthesizing complex ideas. The skills learned in competitive debate prepare students for this type of leadership.

Debate is also a laboratory for effective citizenship in a democratic society. In ancient Greece young men were trained in the arts of speech and debate so they could become effective leaders of the community. Although debate is thought of as a competitive activity, it also prepares students to work together for the common good. Democratic citizens are able to critique the claims of others and argue strongly for causes they passionately believe in.

But as the ancient Greek master Protagoras insisted of his students: If you would be skilled in debating, you must truly understand your opponent's point-of-view and its merits...whether you agree with it or not. This is also the starting-point for a successfully-functioning society.

We believe many political problems in the world today–both foreign and domestic–come from lawmakers' ignoring each other's arguments and simply showcasing their own: Regrettably, we find very little intelligent discussion in the halls of Congress or coming from our various media outlets today.

We sincerely hope this volume will encourage you to become intelligent and articulate advocates for what you believe in. You should accept the fact that you may sometimes be proven wrong. When this happens, you should simply acknowledge that the better argument won out and move on to debate again another day.

Our entire political process would better serve the people if our political figures realized that—although it is important to win an argument—it is equally important to be honest enough to acknowledge when you have been proven wrong.

The whole enterprise only works if we have done our homework. Learning the fundamentals of argumentation is a great way to start.

---

[i] Daniel Goleman, "What Makes a Leader?" *Harvard Business Review*, November-December (1998): 94.

"To find yourself, think for yourself."

—Socrates

About the Authors

Ken Troyer has competed, coached and taught at both high school and collegiate level. A former CEDA debater, Troyer has coached NFL national champions as well as state champions at the high school level and multiple elimination round participants at AFA & NFA national tournament at the collegiate level. Troyer has won the Kansas Speech Communication Association Educator of the year as well as the McCreery Teaching award. Troyer is currently the Assistant Professor of Communication at Sterling College in Sterling, KS.

Gary Harmon has also coached and taught at the high school and collegiate level. With his teams winning multiple state championships, combined with his success at the collegiate level, Gary has recently been recognized by Pi Kappa Delta for more than 50 years of service to the profession. Gary is currently the Debate Coach at Kansas Wesleyan University in Salina, KS.

Dr. David Bailey has had tremendous success in coaching at the collegiate level, with his teams traditionally faring well at the annual Pi Kappa Delta national tournament. Having recently been elected national president of Pi Kappa Delta, Dr. Bailey is committed to maintaining the strength debate programs throughout the US. Dr. Bailey is currently an Assistant Professor of Communication at Southwest Baptist University in Bolivar, MO.

Published by BookRipple
www.BookRipple.com